A MONTH-BY-MONTH GROWING GUIDE FOR BEGINNERS

FEARLESS FOOD GARDENING

in Chicagoland

1st Edition

Authors & Editors
Teresa Gale
LaManda Joy

Contributors
Sally Gregory
Alexandra Nelson
Leah Ray
Lindsay Shepherd
Charlotte Wehr
Stewart Weiss
The volunteer educators of the Peterson Garden Project

Designer
Britta Hernalsteen

Illustrator
Scott Westgard

Printer
Consolidated Printing Company

ISBN: 978-0-9912719-1-7

Peterson Garden Project
4642 N. Francisco Ave.
Chicago, IL 60625
www.petersongarden.org

Printed in the United States by the Peterson Garden Project.
First edition.

Acknowledgements
Thank you to the PGP leadership team, without whom this book (and this program) never would have come to fruition: Maribeth Brewer, Patrick Ewing, Sally Gregory, Mark Kanazawa, Alexandra Nelson, Lester Palmiano, Leah Ray, and Lindsay Shepherd. Thanks to the PGP Board of Directors for their leadership and support: Lester, as well as Rebecca Gerchenson, Erik Kushto, Jason Lundy, and Anjanette Rodrigues. Thanks also to Jason, and to Carla Lee for their assistance with legal matters. And special thanks to our grewbies, whose enthusiasm for food gardening is truly inspiring, and to all of our volunteers who make our program possible.

Writing this Book

My family's roots are in rural Indiana. When I was very young, we moved to the west coast. I grew up in California's central valley at the epicenter of modern "agri-business," but personally disconnected from agriculture. From time to time, my grandma would write me letters about what she was growing in her garden back in Indiana. Corn, beans, kohlrabi. These letters were quaint and endearing, but inconsequential.

In the summers we'd visit my grandparents on the farm. We always ate fresh-picked veggies. I loved inspecting their freezers full of home-grown food. And the basement stock of jams, pickles, and other preserved goods was equally intriguing. It all seemed so foreign.

Years later, I ended up here in Chicago. The summer my husband and I moved into our new home coincided with the birth of our daughter. We now had a small plot of land, and he suggested we start food gardening. In my new-mom stupor, I said something like, "You mean growing our own *vegetables?* That's too much work." But he managed to persuade me otherwise.

I remember feeling so proud of our first harvest. "We did this ourselves!" I marveled. And for the first time, I felt connected to a family history that had always eluded me. Food gardening became truly magical once I saw it through the eyes of my daughter. These special moments — tracing the curve of a pea tendril, hiding in the tomato "forest," watching a butternut squash vine so high we couldn't see the end — have convinced me never to stop.

When LaManda approached me about co-writing a guide to urban food gardening, I didn't know exactly what I was getting into. But I dove in anyway. My short tenure as a food gardener, paired with her lifelong gardening experience, made for an ideal collaboration. We wrote this book together over the course of a year, experiencing in real-time the cycle and discovery of a single growing season. Along the way, we combined what we learned with many of the "best practices" already honed by the Peterson Garden Project's team of educators.

For me, the rewards of food gardening far exceed the work I put into it. I hope you'll feel the same way. I wish you luck, and I'm grateful for the opportunity to share.

Teresa Gale

Welcome to the world of food gardening!

You may think that all you've done is picked up a book. You've actually taken the first step on a journey you can continue for the rest of your life. In fact, once you start food gardening, you just might get hooked and wonder how you ever lived without it!

Sure, you're "ag-curious," as we like to say, but might feel a bit intimidated. Maybe you're thinking, "I can't even keep my house plants alive!" or "My grandma gardened and it seemed complicated. I wish she would have taught me." If food gardening is on your list of fears, or even if you're a bit apprehensive, this book is for you.

Here are a few thoughts to keep in mind as you start on your adventure:

- You'll make mistakes (not just in your first year, but every year) and believe it or not, that's part of the fun.
- Nature will be your best friend ...
- ... and your worst enemy, but getting in synch with the rhythms of nature is a potent antidote to the stress of our technology-centered world.
- Food you grow yourself is the most delicious and satisfying thing ever.

This book is written for beginning gardeners. It gives you the basics, organized month-by-month, and tailored specifically to the Chicago growing region. The advice comes from our own personal gardening experience, and from years of educating thousands of "grewbies" (our name for "newbie" gardeners) through the Peterson Garden Project. This is the book we wish we had as we were starting out.

Thomas Jefferson, founding father and avid food gardener, captured what I love most about gardening when he said, "Though an old man, I am but a young gardener." You never stop learning as a gardener. No two seasons or crops are the same. Gardening can keep us young, and it certainly fills us with joy.

We hope you enjoy your first food gardening experiences, and if you find this book helpful, please let us know. Maybe you'll love growing your own food so much that you'll start to teach others. That would make us very happy, indeed.

LaManda Joy

LaManda Joy
Founder, Peterson Garden Project

Before We Start Digging ...

We'll outline the big picture stuff first. In this chapter, we'll tell you what's unique about gardening in Chicagoland. And we'll share our thoughts on the benefits of food gardening and "organic" gardening, in particular.

Chicago Is Special

If you're new to gardening, you might not realize that a gardening book written for another part of the country could lead you astray. Why? Because geography matters. Climate, frost dates, the built environment, and soil vary from one region to the next, and each of these variables helps determine the gardening character of a particular region.

Here's what's special about Chicago ...

First and foremost: climate. The U.S. is divided into 11 separate "Plant Hardiness Zones" (also referred to as "climate zones") based on average minimum winter temperatures. Gardeners use these zones to determine which plants are likely to thrive in their specific locations. In landscape gardening (as opposed to food gardening), shrubs, perennials, and trees are classified into zones based on the lowest temperatures they can withstand and still continue to grow year after year. There are two zones for the greater Chicago metropolitan area. Most of Cook County resides in zone 6A, and the collar counties (Lake, McHenry, DuPage, Kane, Will and Lake [Indiana]) fall into zone 5B, where temperatures average 5°F colder.

For food gardening, plant hardiness zones are used in combination with "frost dates" to determine the length of the outdoor growing season and planting dates for specific crops. The average last frost date for the Chicago area is April 24th. This means that, on average, April 24th is the last day the temperature drops to 32°. With a few exceptions, most crops can be planted in the ground by this time. Our average first frost date is October 23rd, which marks the close of the growing season (again, with some exceptions — a handful of crops can survive and thrive into the fall and winter). In general, proximity to Lake Michigan means a more temperate climate, so you can probably plant a week or two sooner in the spring and harvest a bit later in the fall if you're close to the lake.

Space (or lack thereof) is a challenge for gardeners in any urban region. Chicago was built up, not out. Much of the city's residential core was constructed prior to World War II, before suburbs became the American ideal. The city itself is much denser than surrounding communities. Residential lots in Chicago are quite small — typically 125' x 25', with homes and detached garages occupying much of the lot area. Perhaps you have a sunny spot in your backyard, or access to a community garden plot. Either way, it probably doesn't allow for a sprawling vegetable garden. You'll want to use your space efficiently, and we'll help you find ways to do this.

Average Annual Extreme Minimum Temperature
1976 to 2005

Temp (F)	ZONE	Temp (C)
-20 to -15	5a	-28.9 to -26.1
-15 to -10	5b	-26.1 to -23.3
-10 to -5	6a	-23.3 to -20.6
-5 to 0	6b	-20.6 to -17.8
0 to 5	7a	-17.8 to -15.0

U.S. Department of Agriculture

Agricultural Research Service

Mapping by the PRISM Climate Group
Oregon State University

Source: http://planthardiness.ars.usda.gov/PHZMWeb/Maps.aspx

Whether you live in a high-rise, single-family, or multi-unit home, you're likely pretty close to your neighbors. The density and height of buildings can often create shady conditions that are not ideal for food gardening. On the plus side, built structures can also retain heat and create "micro-climates" that are beneficial and may actually accelerate your harvest and lengthen your growing season. As you progress as a gardener, you'll learn to identify these local factors and use them to your advantage.

Chicago has a long history of industry and manufacturing. As a result, "city soil" and its potential for contaminants are a reality that we urban gardeners have to face. Not to worry—we'll teach you tried and true methods for controlling the composition of your soil and ensuring the health and quality of the food that you grow.

Benefits of Food Gardening

Homegrown food is better. You probably already know this, but at the risk of preaching to the choir, we'll elaborate.

The longer produce is in transit from farm to marketplace to consumer, the more likely it is to lose flavor and nutritional value. By growing food yourself, you're opting out of the industrial food supply chain. Food from your own backyard is fresher, healthier, and tastes better than the store-bought kind. It's as local as you can get.

A local food system works to minimize "food miles," or how far food has traveled from its origin to the consumer. Eating "locally" means obtaining your food, or as much of it as you can, from a radius close to home. A local food radius can be 50, 100, 250 miles, or anywhere in between (there's no agreed upon standard). Reducing food miles lowers greenhouse gas emissions, and supporting local farms and local food production helps build more self- reliant, sustainable food economies.

Food gardening also can be beneficial to your health, both physically and emotionally. The act of gardening itself is a form of low impact exercise, and it can relieve stress (it's even prescribed as therapy in some circumstances). It can build friendships, strengthen family bonds, and encourage cultural preservation, as elders teach food traditions to younger friends and family members, who in turn pass them down to the next generation.

Did we mention you save money? The expenses you incur with your initial garden set-up will be recouped quickly. After your first season, year-to-year maintenance and planting costs are relatively minimal. Remember, when you buy a vegetable in a store, you're paying the costs of harvesting, storing, and transporting it. By growing your own, you avoid these costs. You'll spend an average of $1–3 per seed packet, and many packets will last you more than one season. If you plant from young plants instead of seeds, you'll spend just a few dollars per plant. A single tomato plant can yield anywhere from 5–20 pounds of fruit... you do the math!

Organic Gardening 101

We're proponents of organic gardening and have written this book from our perspective as organic gardeners. Our goal is to help you grow your own food in a healthy, sustainable way, and the best approach for this, we believe, is to use organic gardening techniques.

So what exactly is "organic" gardening? It's a practice that supports the long-term health of soil, plants, ecosystems, and people. It means working with nature, conserving garden resources, and promoting "biodiversity," or variety in all forms of life—plants, animals, and microorganisms. The more variety, the healthier the ecosystem.

As an organic gardener, your most important job is care of the soil. The less you tinker with your soil, the more fertile it will be. Millions of organisms (earthworms, fungi, algae, microscopic bacteria, etc.) are at work in healthy soil, creating, storing, and distributing essential nutrients. You can protect and help nurture these creatures by minimizing disturbances to them. Avoid turning and tilling, which can disrupt the complex, balanced ecosystem that's already in place and result in soil degradation and erosion. And don't walk on your soil, because you'll compact it and collapse air pockets needed to move water and oxygen to plants.

In the process of building and maintaining healthy soil, you'll need to add organic matter on a regular basis. Compost, also known as "black gold," is organic matter such as vegetable scraps, yard waste, and manure that has decomposed over a period of weeks or months and broken down into a crumbly soil-like texture. Adding compost to your soil replenishes nutrients, improves the soil's ability to hold air and water, and promotes good drainage. Compost serves as food and nourishment for all the organisms in your soil. It's the most essential ingredient in organic soil.

OMRI

When you're shopping for organic gardening products, check for the OMRI® label. This means they've been reviewed by the Organic Materials Review Institute to ensure compliance with USDA organic standards. You can also check for OMRI® listed products online at www.omri.org.

OMRI
For Organic Use

Your soil will stay fertile and won't require chemical or synthetic fertilizers, so long as you nurture and attend to it. And the healthier your soil is, the less likely you are to encounter pests and disease in your garden. Still, unwanted guests might pay a visit from time to time. Organic approaches to pest and disease management (detailed in the June section of this guide) are effective alternatives to using pesticides and herbicides, which can kill good organisms as well as bad ones.

Crop diversity — that is, growing the greatest variety of plants that you can — helps create and sustain a healthy garden ecosystem. Each plant that you grow (non-edibles included) provides habitat and food for different creatures. The more varieties you grow, the more opportunities you provide for complex interactions to take place. This doesn't mean you have to plant 20 different kinds of veggies if you don't have the space. But do plant some of your favorites and include a few annuals and perennials in the mix (many flowers are edible, too!). And make sure to experiment with something new from time to time.

Raised Beds

Because soil contents are critical to the health of your garden, we recommend planting above the ground in what's called a "raised bed" and filling the bed with new, clean soil. So this means not planting in the ground. If your yard consists of concrete or another impermeable surface, this is probably welcome news — yes, you can grow vegetables, even if you don't have "land"!

Simply put, a raised bed is a box full of soil. It's usually square or rectangular and fairly small, ranging anywhere from 2' x 2' to 3' x 5' to 4' x 8'. Raised beds are most often built out of wood, but sometimes other materials such as concrete blocks or bricks are used.

The main advantage of a raised bed is control over your soil. By making your own soil mix and containing it above the ground, you can be sure it's contaminant-free, plus you bypass the process of soil improvement and conditioning typically necessary for in-ground planting. In addition, soil in a raised bed drains better than in-ground soil, and it warms up quickly in the spring, so you can start planting your crops earlier than you'd be able to in the ground.

Raised beds also provide you more space efficiency than you'd have with traditional farm-style row planting. When you plant in rows, you need to allow several feet of space in between rows to walk back and forth and access crops. With raised beds, you reach in from the outside to access crops, and your soil mix provides optimal conditions for deep root development, so you can plant crops closer together than you would in the ground. Raised beds are a compact and economical use of space. And they give you flexibility, as you can locate individual boxes in more than one place throughout the yard.

We advise situating raised beds at ground level. This isn't to say you can't install one on your deck, balcony or other above-ground structure. Just make sure that before you build, you research the load-bearing capacity of the structure to confirm it can support the weight of a garden bed. Or consider using smaller containers that can be positioned separately, with weight distributed more evenly over the structure.

Gardening in Containers

If your outdoor space is really limited, or if you live in a multi-unit building where you're not allowed to install a raised bed, you might feel tempted to put this book down right about now.

Don't be discouraged! Containers (pots, troughs, hanging baskets, etc.) are a perfectly fine alternative to raised beds, and they offer you the same control over your soil as a raised bed. You'll be surprised at the amount of food you can grow in pots on your patio, porch, balcony, or roof. Even if you have room for a raised bed, you can still supplement with containers. A pot or trough can always be nestled here or there, so no space is left to waste.

Rest assured — most of the instruction in our month-by-month guide can be applied to container gardening. *So please read on!*

January + February

It's no secret: winter in Chicago is daunting. By January, the holiday frenzy has subsided and cold weather has settled in for the long haul. You're stuck indoors most of the time, daydreaming about warmer temperatures. But hope springs eternal as the days go by. Now is an opportune time to imagine and plan your garden.

Your imaginary garden will be much bigger than your real garden (this is a phenomenon that never seems to wear off, no matter how long you garden). Spend some time browsing seed catalogs to inspire and help visualize what you can grow. You may end up buying too many seeds, but you can always save them for next year or share them with friends (gardening makes people generous).

Winter is a great time to become part of a "seed swapping" group. Chances are someone else has found an interesting or rare vegetable you've never heard of (purple carrots, cinnamon basil, lemon cucumbers ... mmm). Before you know it, your brain is overflowing with yummy ideas that will sustain you for a couple more months, until you can start digging in the soil.

In this section, we'll teach you how to get started from square one. We'll tell you what tools you'll need and help you situate your garden bed so it's convenient and bountiful. We'll also educate you on seed terminology so you'll be well informed when you start to shop.

Okay ... here we go!

Getting Started

First things first. Take an inventory of your garden resources. Survey your garage, basement, or storage area for tools and containers (even if you're planning for a raised bed, it's nice to have a few pots available for herbs or extra plants that won't fit into your bed). Clean and organize what you already have and make a note of what you'll need to buy.

You can save money and add visual interest by repurposing things that you don't normally think of as garden containers — cooking pots, wooden crates, barrels, cinder blocks, plastic storage bins, metal and porcelain sinks — to name a few. Be creative. Just make sure not to use anything with chemical residue that could leach into your soil, and if there aren't already holes in the bottom for drainage, go ahead and drill some.

TOOL LIST

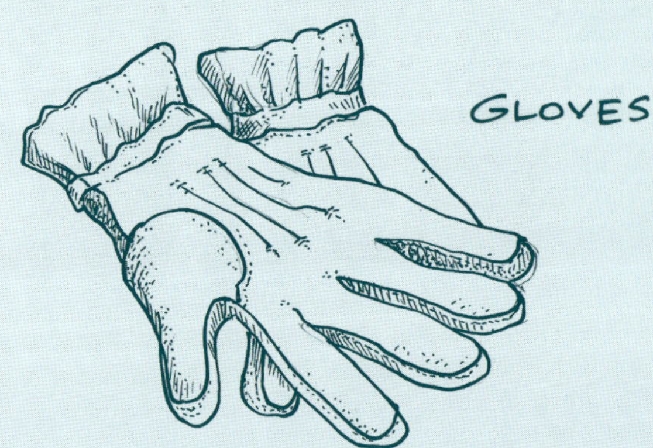

GLOVES

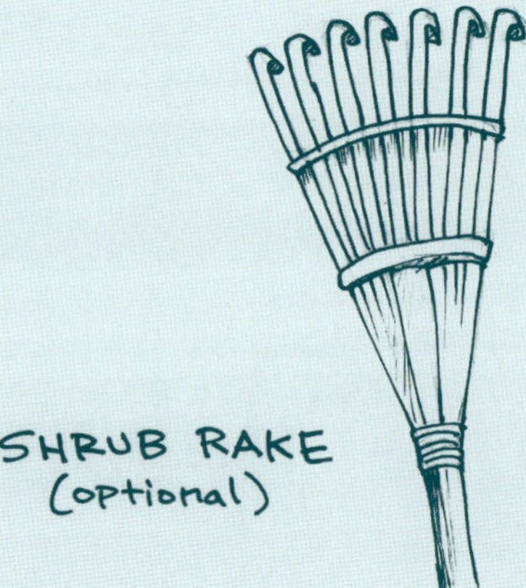

SHRUB RAKE
(optional)

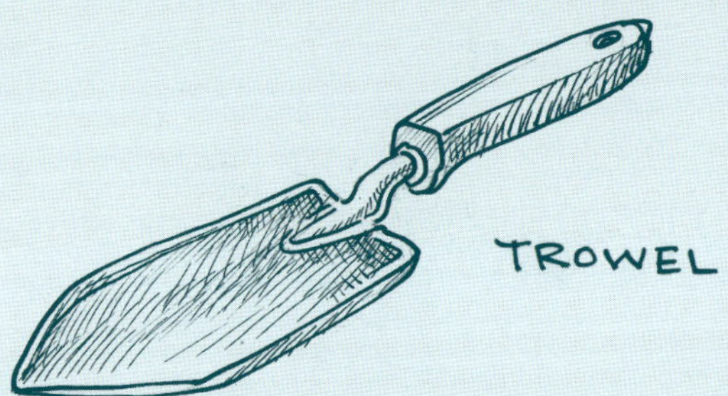

TROWEL

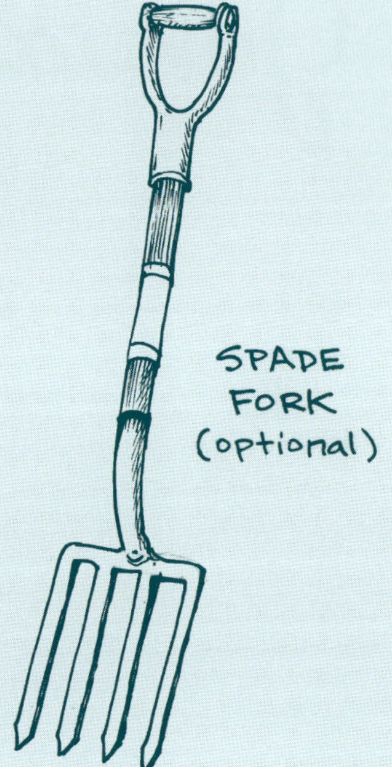

SPADE
FORK
(optional)

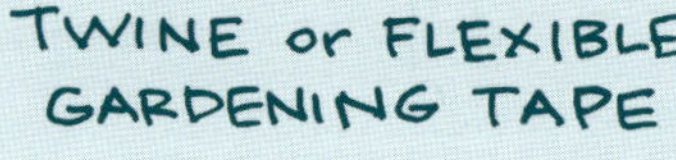

TWINE or FLEXIBLE
GARDENING TAPE

SCISSORS or
PRUNING SHEARS

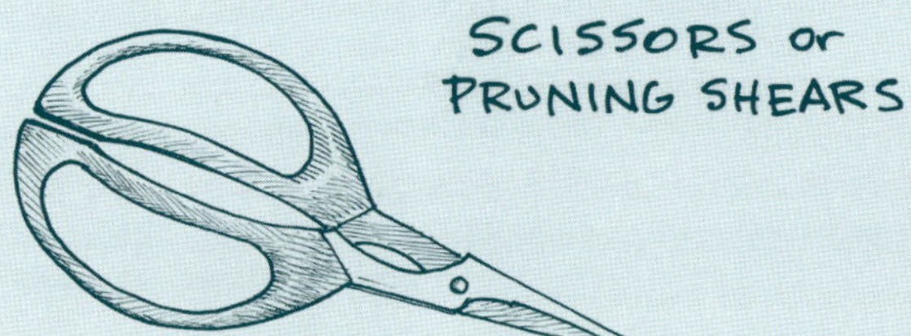

KNEELING PAD
(optional)

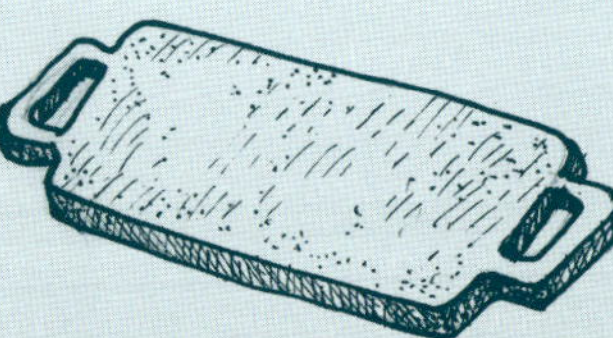

WATERING DEVICE
(watering can with rose attachment or hose with wand/spray nozzle)

Location, Location, Location

Take a look at your outdoor space. Chances are it's covered in snow, or maybe it's just bare and brown. If you have some photographs from last spring or summer, consult them to remind yourself of what the area looks like in full bloom. Try your best to envision how it will look in a few months.

Location is critical, so consider it very carefully. Most crops need "full sun" in order to thrive, which means 6 or more hours of direct sunlight a day. Less sun will slow plant growth, and you don't have much time to spare in Chicago's short growing season. Still, some vegetables can do well in "part sun," meaning 2–4 hours of morning or midday sun, and others will tolerate dappled shade under a tree or lattice. If you don't have any access to sunlight, then you're probably better off gardening in a community garden (see our Resources section for information on how to get connected).

As you're scouting for a location, keep in mind that sun exposure varies significantly throughout the year. In mid-winter, the sun is much lower in the sky than it is in summertime. Areas that are now blanketed in shade might actually enjoy full sun at the height of summer. Observe how the sun

CROPS FOR PART SUN (2–4 HOURS)

- Chives
- Cilantro
- Leafy greens
- Parsley
- Peas
- Scallions

CROPS FOR DAPPLED SUN

- Beet greens
- Cabbage (small headed varieties)
- Endive
- Leeks
- Lettuce
- Radishes
- Spinach
- Turnip greens

moves through your yard over the course of a day, then project where your sunniest spot will be. Areas facing the south will have more exposure, and the more sun the better.

Whether you plant in the front, back, or to the side of your home is up to you. Planting in the back of your home will probably give you the most space and privacy. While the city of Chicago has no law that prohibits edible plantings in your front yard, you may find it challenging due to limited space and the potential for veggie theft (unless you have a fenced or enclosed area). If you live outside of Chicago and want to confirm that front yard planting is permitted, check with your local zoning authority. Side yards, also called "gang-ways," can be quite narrow and shaded for much of the day, depending on the height of neighboring buildings. But don't rule them out — the exposure they do get might be strong sun, and a few hours of this can be enough to grow a variety of vegetables.

Survey your yard for potential "microclimates" that might impact your growing conditions. A microclimate is a small area whose climate is affected by local factors such as exposure to sun or wind, slope of land, and proximity to structures. For example, a broad open area will have more wind exposure. A low-lying area will attract cold air and may be more prone to frost, as well as poor drainage. Locating your garden near the foundation of your house or garage can provide added warmth and shelter from wind, and will likely extend your growing season a bit. Planting near a tree or large shrub can help protect from wind and cold, but the tree might shade your garden more than you'd like. In addition, tree and shrub roots can sense well watered soil nearby, grow toward it, and potentially interfere with your bed over time.

Situate your garden in a place that's convenient to you — preferably somewhere close to the house or garage. You'll be more attentive to an area that you see and pass by regularly. It also should be near your water supply and tools, which you'll need to use on a daily basis. You want gardening to be an enjoyable experience, not a chore.

The Truth About Seeds

Seed varieties abound, and there's often confusion about which varieties are best. Maybe you've heard terms such as "GMO" or "heirloom," but aren't completely sure what they mean. You'll want to have a basic understanding of these and other terms before you set out to buy seeds. Our goal is to help you make educated decisions about what's best for your garden, so we'll clarify some common terms that you're likely to encounter.

The terms "GE" (Genetically Engineered) and "GMO" (Genetically Modified Organism) are often used interchangeably, but do not mean the same thing. Genetic engineering is the scientific practice of incorporating genes directly into an organism by way of recombinant DNA techniques. GE plants do not occur in nature, but are a product of human intervention. As a home gardener, you won't find GE seeds in seed catalogs or garden centers. Presently GE techniques are used only in large-scale agriculture, and are the subject of ongoing ethical debate.

A GMO is an organism produced by any means of genetic modification, whether by modern genetic engineering or age-old plant breeding methods. For thousands of years, plant breeders have manipulated organisms to improve quality and productivity, making the same kinds of selections that can also occur in nature. Seedless watermelon and pluots are examples of modern GMOs.

A "hybrid" is created when a breeder cross-pollinates two pure plant lines to produce a seed with desirable traits — such as disease resistance, uniformity, or color — from both parents. Popular home garden hybrids include Sungold and Better Boy tomatoes. Production methods for hybrids are highly controlled and must remain consistent from one year to the next. Seeds can be saved and planted from hybrids, but there's no guarantee that plants grown from these seeds will contain the desirable characteristics of the parent plants.

On the other hand, seeds that are saved from "open-pollinated" varieties and then planted in subsequent years will produce plants with the same characteristics of the parent plant. Open-pollination occurs naturally, without human intervention, via insects, wind, or self-pollination (when both male and female flowers reside on the same plant). The term "heirloom" describes any open-pollinated variety existing prior to the 1940s and 50s, when plant breeders began producing modern hybrids. As the name suggests, many heirloom varieties have been passed down through generations of gardeners. Heirloom seeds, like hybrid ones, are grown on a commercial scale and sold to seed distribution companies.

Any seed packet labeled "Certified Organic" has been produced in strict accordance with the USDA's National Organic Program. Organic seeds are grown without the use of synthetic fertilizers and pesticides, sewage sludge,

SEED LIFESPAN FOR POPULAR CROPS

Crop	Lifespan
Corn, onions	1-2 years
Chives, okra, parsley	2-3 years
Beans, carrots, peas	3-4 years
Beets, peppers, Swiss chard, tomatoes	4-5 years
Basil, broccoli, cabbage, cauliflower, cucumber, eggplant, lettuce, melon, radishes, spinach, squash	5-6 years

SEEDS WITH STORIES: THE GROUND CHERRY

Organizations like Seed Savers Exchange have collected heirloom seeds since the mid-1970s. They work to preserve the genetic traits of plants (such as disease resistance or drought tolerance) and promote genetic diversity, which helps maintain a safe and productive food supply.

Genetics aside, heirloom seeds are an important means of cultural preservation. Many of them are passed down from one generation to the next and tell stories of immigration, settlement, movement and hope. Heirloom plants give new gardeners a taste of the past and a link to stories that are compelling and culturally rich.

Take the ground cherry, for example. Ground cherries were ubiquitous in home gardens a century ago. The fruit—closer in relation to tomatillos than actual cherries—was eaten fresh and in pies and preserves. As agriculture became more mechanized, these delicate fruits were not suitable for large-scale growing and shipping, and they fell out of favor. By growing them in your home garden, you'll have the opportunity to taste a flavor you may not recognize (but will surely enjoy) and revive recipes from long ago. And you'll have a great story to share with your friends and neighbors!

irradiation, and genetic engineering. In addition, the land on which organic crops are grown cannot have had prohibited substances applied for three years prior to harvest.

Do you have to buy organic seeds? No. When it comes to organic gardening, how you raise the plant once it's growing matters more than using organic seeds. Organizations that raise organic seeds are doing good work and need support. But if that special variety you want is only available as a conventionally raised seed, then by all means, get it!

Most seed packets contain more than enough seeds for one season, so don't feel obligated to plant a whole packet at one time. Plant only what you need and save the rest for next year. Seeds can last up to five years if stored properly. They're best stored in their original packet inside of an airtight container, away from warmth and humidity (avoiding humidity is more important than avoiding heat). Germination rates of stored seeds will gradually decrease over time, but you can compensate for this by planting a few seeds instead of just one to ensure that at least one seed will sprout.

Phew. That's a lot of information on seeds! But we think you deserve to know it. We advocate buying seed varieties that are rare, organic, or open-pollinated whenever possible. When you're ready to buy, peruse your local nursery as well as online and print seed catalogs, which tend to offer a wide selection and hard-to-find varieties.

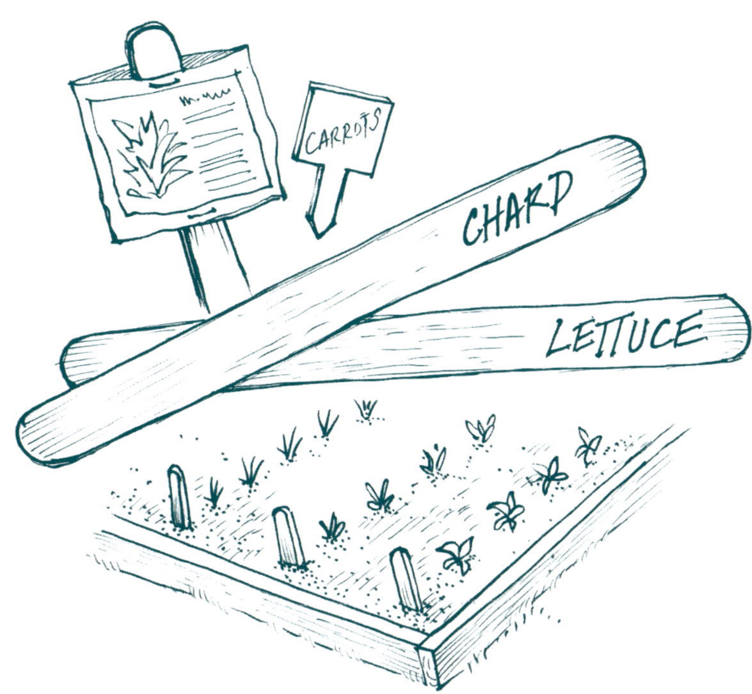

March

Winter is coming to an end (we hope—it's March after all, and March is unpredictable). You've decided where to put your garden and about what size it will be. The next question is: what to grow? Our advice to any gardener, whether beginner or experienced, is to grow what you want to eat.

Now is the time to buy seeds, if you haven't already. This month we'll give you ideas on which crops to choose, and identify ones that are best started from young plants rather than seeds. We'll explain the difference between "cool" and "hot" season crops. And we'll help you organize your plantings within your raised bed to maximize space and productivity.

(If the weather is mild and you feel motivated, you might skip ahead to April and get started building your bed!)

What to Grow

As you ponder what to plant, time and space will be your main considerations. Since our growing season in Chicago is relatively short, we recommend focusing on high-yield and continuous-yield crops, such as tomatoes, beans, peppers, and leafy greens, which will continue to produce a harvest throughout much of the season. These crops will net you the most for the space they occupy.

Be selective about planting space-hogging crops like squash, melons, and cucumbers. They'll grow rapidly and produce creeping vines that can easily take over your garden. The best way to accommodate a vining plant is to grow "up" rather than out. This means securing the vine to a vertical structure such as a trellis, cage, fence, or even a tree, as it grows. Gardening vertically saves a lot of space. Keep in mind that a plant attached to a vertical structure will cast a shadow. So make sure not to plant sun-loving crops too close to a trellis—at least not directly to the north where they'll be shaded.

Is it really worth it to grow a watermelon? We'll let you be the judge. If you're growing food to save money, you can measure a crop's value in terms of price per pound, keeping in mind that vegetable prices vary depending on region, season, and where you shop. You can also determine value by how much a crop yields relative to the space it takes up. Of course, taste buds and sentiment might win out over economics. It's always okay to grow something for the sheer joy of growing it. So even though potatoes may be cheaper to buy than grow, they're sure fun to dig up come harvest time!

Seeds or Seedlings?

Seeds vary in terms of how long they take to "germinate," or sprout, and grow into mature plants. For instance, radishes typically take 4 weeks to grow from seed to harvest. In contrast, tomatoes take about 17 weeks, and eggplants and peppers take 19 weeks.

While you can start any crop from seeds planted directly in the ground, for crops that mature slowly, we suggest purchasing a "seedling," or young plant, from a local nursery and transplanting it into your garden. Our growing season isn't long enough to accommodate the full life cycle of most slow-maturing crops. By starting with a seedling, you can speed up your harvest by at least a few weeks. If you're curious to know how many weeks old your seedling is, nursery staff should be able to tell you.

Some experienced gardeners start their seeds indoors prior to the outdoor growing season, and then transplant the seedlings outside once the weather permits. "Seed starting," as the process is often called, is not something you need to worry about as a new gardener. After you get a couple seasons under your belt, you might give it a try (see the Beyond the Basics chapter to learn more about the process).

LIFE CYCLE FOR POPULAR CROPS

Crop	Average Weeks to Maturity
Cress, mustard greens, radishes	4-5
Arugula, beans ("bush" varieties), beets, lettuce, swiss chard, tatsoi	6-8
Endive, kale, spinach, summer squash, zucchini	7-8
Cucumbers, peas	8-10
Corn	9-13
Beans ("pole" varieties), carrots, peas, turnips	10
Basil, melon, okra, pumpkins, winter squash	12
Cauliflower, parsley	14
Broccoli, cabbage, chives	16
Tomatoes	17
Eggplant, peppers	19

Garden Layout

As you're finalizing your plant list, you'll need to consider how much space each plant will take up once it reaches mature size. This can be hard to judge if you've never grown vegetables, or if you've only seen them in the supermarket, trimmed of excess foliage. Vegetable size doesn't necessarily correspond to the size of its parent plant. For instance, okra pods are quite small, but an okra plant can grow over 4 feet tall and 3 feet wide.

Once you become familiar with your plant sizes, you can start planning a layout for your raised bed. An effective technique is to divide your bed into a grid, with each square measuring one square foot, and then organize your plantings per square foot. So if you have 12 square feet, you'll have 12 squares in which to plant.

But you won't necessarily have 12 plants — in fact, you may have more. Plant spacing is determined by mature plant size, which varies widely. Cabbage and tomato plants, for example, are large and should be allotted one square foot each, at minimum. On the other hand, beets and spinach are small and can be planted up to 9 per square foot. This method of planting is often called "intensive" because it yields high productivity in such a small space.

When situating your plants, visualize them in three dimensions as they grow up and out. Your cabbage plant might grow 1 – 2 feet wide, but stay compact and low-lying at only 6 – 18 inches tall. In contrast, your tomato plant could grow many feet in height and sprawl outward, potentially shading nearby plants (your spinach might benefit from this shade, but your beets will need full sun). Consider the growth habit and sun requirements of each plant, and plan accordingly.

Now is a good time to sketch out a simple garden map (use a pencil — you'll probably change your mind a lot!). This will be your guide as you start planting, and it will be especially handy when plants are young and it's hard to identify what's what. Your map will also serve as a historical reference for future garden planning.

If you want to take a hi-tech approach to mapping, visit the Gardener's Supply Company web site (www.gardeners.com) for a fantastic tool called the Kitchen Garden Planner. It allows you to custom design and print a map for your raised bed, and also offers planting instructions for each vegetable you choose.

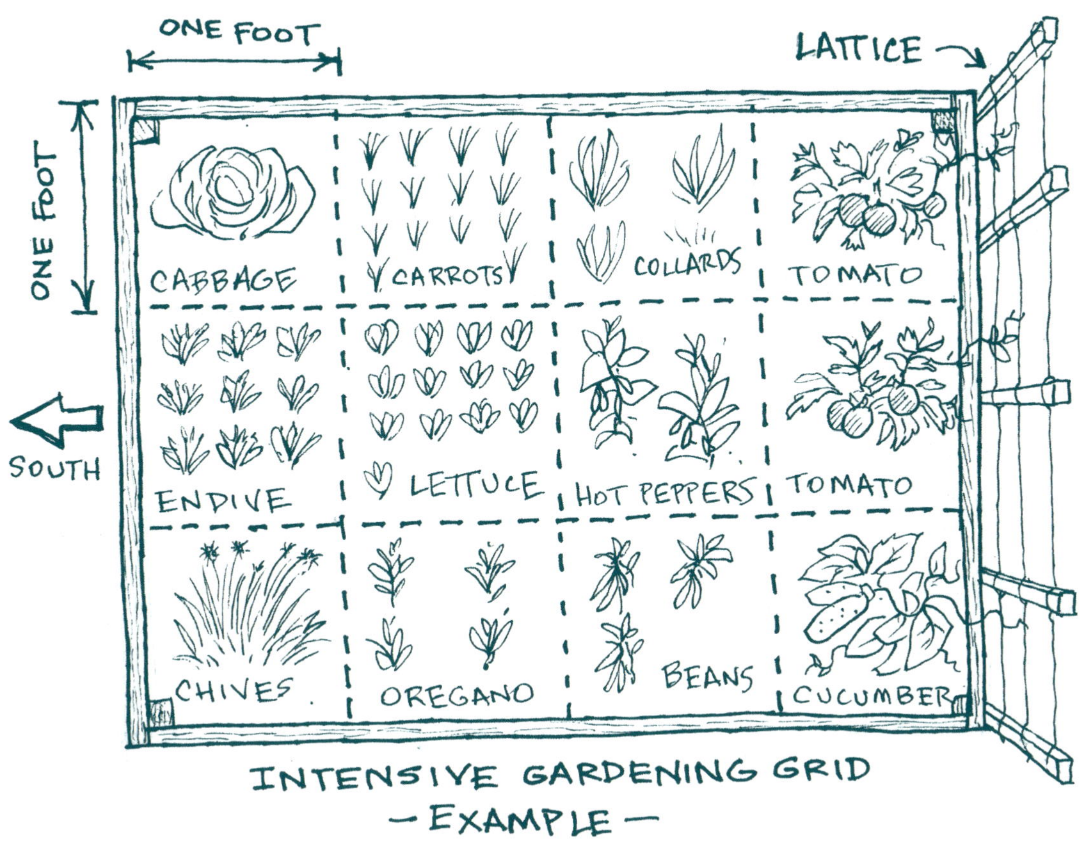

MORE BANG FOR YOUR BUCK

(high value for the amount of space they take up—typically cheaper to grow than buy)

- Arugula
- Asparagus
- Basil
- Beans
- Beets (greens and roots)
- Cucumbers
- Eggplant
- Kale
- Lettuce
- Mint
- Onions
- Parsley
- Peppers
- Radishes
- Rhubarb
- Scallions
- Summer squash
- Swiss chard
- Tomatoes
- Turnips (greens and roots)
- Zucchini

LESS BANG FOR YOUR BUCK

(low value for the amount of space they take up—typically cheaper to buy than grow)

- Broccoli
- Cabbage
- Cauliflower
- Corn
- Melons
- Potatoes
- Pumpkins
- Winter squash

CROPS THAT ARE EASY TO GROW IN CONTAINERS

- Basil (and other herbs)
- Blueberries
- Lettuce
- Peppers
- Radishes
- Swiss chard
- Strawberries
- Tomatoes ("determinate" varieties, which top out at 3–5 feet tall)

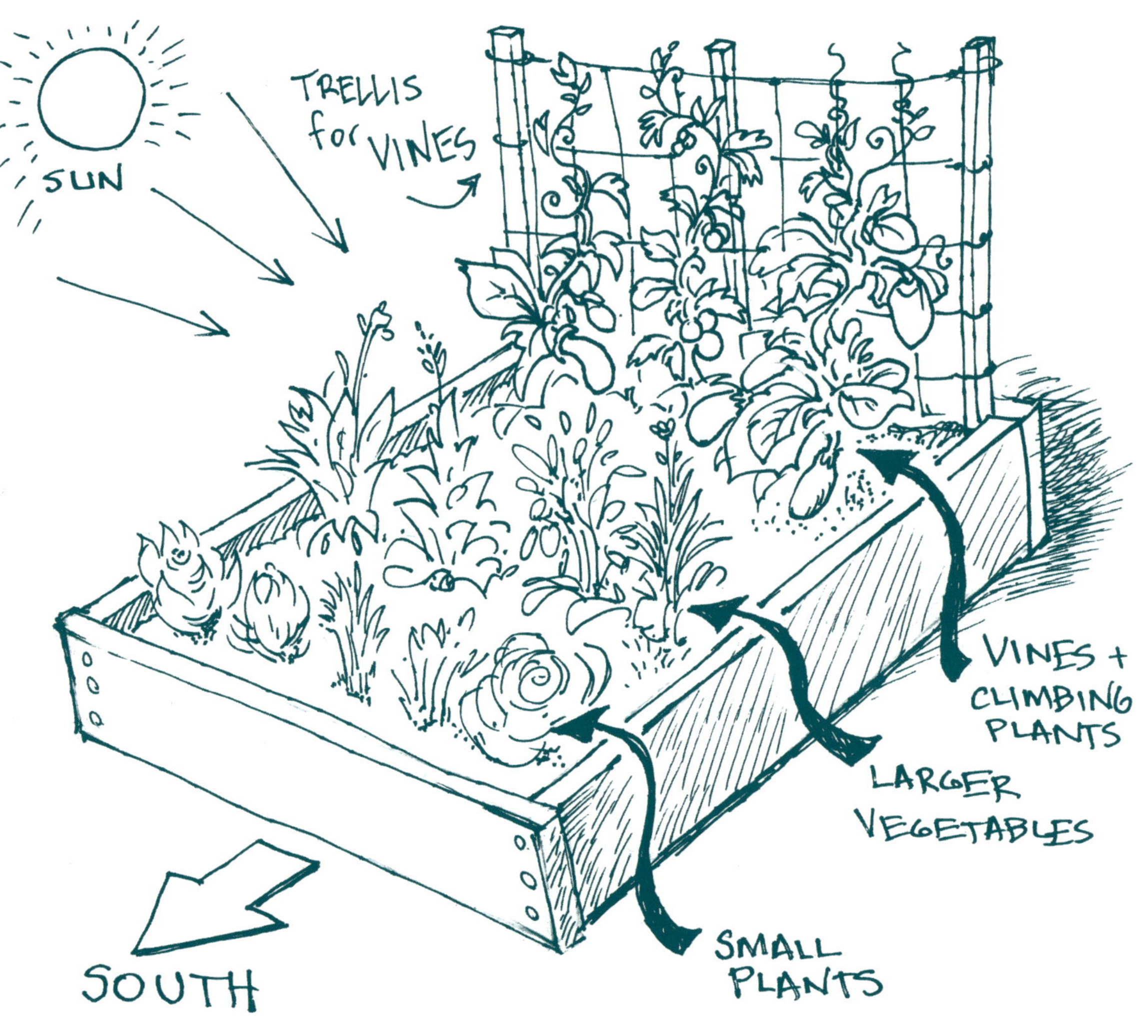

PLANT SIZES AT FULL MATURITY

Small

- Beets
- Carrots
- Chives
- Cilantro
- Endive
- Garlic
- Leeks
- Lettuce
- Onions
- Parsley
- Parsnips
- Radishes
- Spinach
- Turnips

Medium

- Basil
- Collards
- Eggplant
- Kale
- Lavender
- Oregano
- Peppers (hot)
- Rosemary
- Sage
- Swiss chard

Large

- Beans
- Broccoli
- Brussels sprouts
- Cabbage
- Cauliflower
- Corn
- Cucumbers
- Melons
- Okra
- Peas
- Peppers (bell, poblano)
- Potatoes
- Pumpkins
- Summer squash
- Sunflowers
- Tomatillos
- Tomatoes
- Winter squash
- Zucchini

When to Plant

Whether you're planting from seeds or seedlings, you won't be putting everything in the ground at the same time. Air and soil temperatures will determine when to plant your crops.

Chicago's growing season can be divided into three sub-seasons: cool (spring), hot (summer), and cool (fall).

	Cool Season (Spring and Fall)	Hot Season (Summer)
Required soil temperature for seed germination	45 - 55°	55 - 65°
Required air temperature for plant growth	40 - 60°	60° or above
Recommended crops	• Beets • Broccoli • Brussels sprouts • Cabbage • Carrots • Cauliflower • Celery • Chives • Kohlrabi • Lavender • Leafy greens • Onions • Parsley • Parsnips • Peas • Potatoes • Radishes • Turnips	• Basil • Beans • Corn • Cucumbers • Eggplant • Melons • Okra • Peppers • Pumpkins • Summer squash • Sweet potatoes • Tomatoes • Winter squash • Zucchini

Once your initial crops are spent or past their peak, you can replace them right away with new seeds or seedlings as temperatures allow (the soil doesn't need down time). For example, when your spring greens are done, plant tomatoes in their place, and so on. This method of planting one-right-after-the-next, called "succession" planting, maximizes production and makes efficient use of the space in your raised bed.

Edible Perennials

Most vegetables are "annuals" that complete their life cycle in one season and require replanting every year. However, a few vegetables, and many herbs and fruits, are "perennials" that die back in the fall and sprout up again in the spring on their own. Here are some popular perennial crops:

- Asparagus
- Blackberries
- Blueberries
- Bunching onions
- Chives
- Jerusalem artichokes (sunchokes)
- Lavender
- Mint
- Raspberries
- Rhubarb
- Sage
- Sorrel
- Strawberries

Edible perennials are a worthwhile investment. Favorites such as rhubarb and asparagus take a couple seasons to establish themselves, but can produce for many years (even decades). Perennials will need a permanent location within your raised bed, or maybe even a bed of their own, so take some extra time to consider them when planning your garden layout.

GARDENING WITH KIDS

Kids are natural gardeners. They're curious, energetic, and love to play in the soil. When kids work in the garden, they learn firsthand about cycles of life and experience the reward of nurturing something over time. And if they grow vegetables, they're more likely to eat them.

Here are some kid-tested crops that are easy to grow, mature quickly, or are just plain fun to harvest!

- Beans ("bush" varieties)
- Carrots
- Cherry tomatoes
- Mesclun lettuce
- Peas
- Potatoes
- Pumpkins
- Radishes
- Strawberries
- Sunflowers

POTATOES

Potatoes are some of the earliest crops you can plant in the spring—and some of the easiest to grow. According to Chicago folklore, you can plant them as soon as St. Patrick's Day. So even though we advise waiting until April to plant most crops, feel free to start a bit earlier with your spuds.

First you'll need to buy "seed" potatoes, which are actually small potatoes, from a seed company or reputable garden center. If you're really eager to get them in the ground, look for "early season" varieties, which are planted and harvested sooner than mid- and late season ones.

You can plant your tubers whole or cut them into several pieces before planting. Make sure each piece has an "eye," or dimple—this is where it will start to sprout. While it's true that you can simply plant any old potato in the ground, we recommend avoiding supermarket varieties, which are often treated with growth inhibitors to prevent them from sprouting.

Some gardeners prepare their seed potatoes by "chitting" them, or leaving them in a cool, light place for a few weeks to encourage them to sprout. We think this step is unnecessary, since potatoes are such enthusiastic growers.

SEED POTATOES

When you're ready to plant, dig holes in your soil about 4 inches deep and 12 inches apart. Then drop in your tubers and cover them with soil. As the plants grow, you'll need to "hill" them by mounding up the soil around the stems. So once the foliage reaches about 8 inches tall, hill the plants until just a few leaves are visible on top. Repeat this step once they've grown another 8 inches. Potatoes will form along the buried stems.

Needless to say, things can get a little messy in the hilling process. Your standard 6-inch raised bed might not accommodate all this extra soil. Consider building a taller bed just for potatoes, or use an enclosure such as a whiskey barrel, or a bushel or laundry basket with the bottom removed. Feel free to get creative. Just make sure you plan ahead.

PLANT SEED POTATO

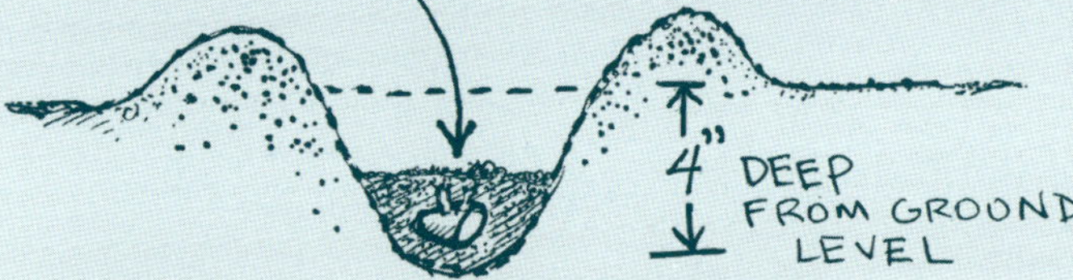

AS THE PLANT GROWS, "HILL" MORE SOIL OVER IT

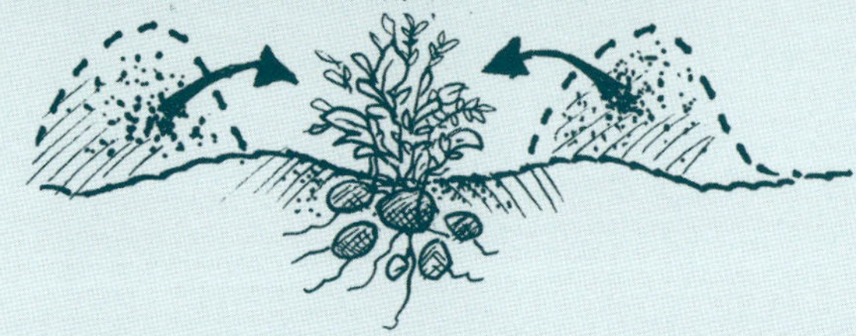

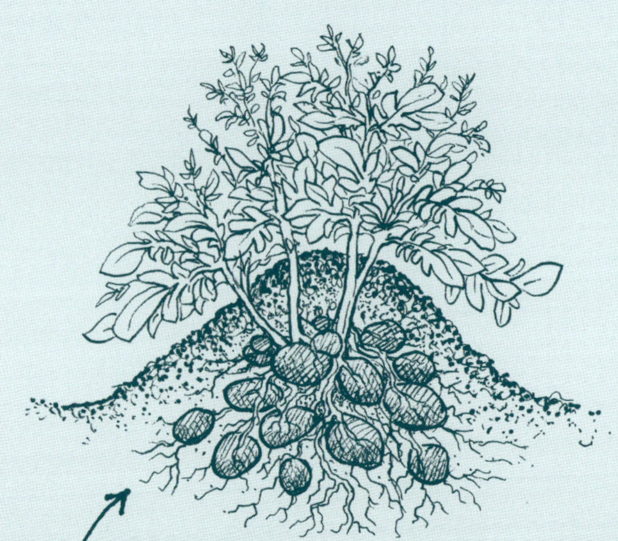

POTATOES FORM ON BURIED STEMS

April

Oh, April! With more nice days to play outside, you can finally get your hands dirty. Now you'll really start gardening in earnest. You'll get acquainted with cool season crops — those tasty, hopeful veggies that don't mind a little chill as they're growing. Maybe you've been talking with friends about your new project and they're craving homegrown produce, too (you might even enlist their help!).

This month we'll give you step-by-step instructions on how to build your raised bed and mix your soil. We'll explain how to plant seeds, as well as how to transplant seedlings you buy from a nursery.

And we'll provide ideas for pest-proofing. We hate to break it to you, but we have urban critters — rabbits, squirrels, and yes, even rats — that sometimes like our gardens as much as we do (even so, don't let a few pests dissuade you from growing your own food!).

April is known for its showers. Chances are Mother Nature will do some of the watering and you'll need to fill in the gaps. We'll teach you the best watering methods for your plants as they sprout and grow into maturity. And while our average last frost date is April 24th, light freezes are still a possibility. Not to worry — we'll introduce a few simple devices you can use to protect sensitive crops in the event of a late frost.

Building Your Bed

Time to build your raised bed! The dimensions are up to you. Remember, make it no wider than 4 feet, or 3 feet if you're going to situate it against a wall or fence. This way you can reach in comfortably from the outside without having to step on your beautiful organic soil. Lumber comes in 8- and 10-foot lengths and can be cut by the lumber supplier, usually free of charge.

If you're using materials other than wood, such as concrete blocks or bricks, the construction process is straightforward: line them up and stack them straight. The bed's walls should be at least 6 inches in height to contain your soil and provide enough room for plants to grow. You can build your bed taller if you like, regardless of what materials you're using. Just be prepared to fill it with more soil.

MATERIALS

- 4 wood boards (2 for the long sides, 2 for the short sides), cut to your preferred length
- 4 corner posts, cut to the same height as the boards
- Deck screws (twice as long as the board thickness)
- Power drill
- Weed cloth (or other weed barrier, like cardboard)
- Organic soil
- Organic compost

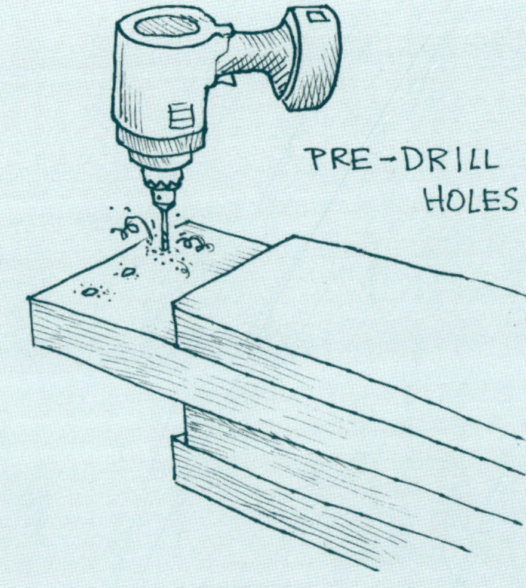

ASSEMBLY

Assemble your frame on a hard, level surface—like your garage floor or sidewalk—so it doesn't end up bowed or crooked.

Step 1: Using a drill bit that's a little smaller in diameter than your screw, pre-drill 2–3 holes into the end of each board (this helps prevent the wood from splitting when you drive in the screws). Have a board or two underneath the one you're drilling to keep your drill bit from hitting the ground when it pokes through the wood.

Step 2: Put together the short sides of your frame first. Position the end of your board against a corner post and screw the pieces together. Screw a second corner post into the opposite end. Repeat for the other short side.

Step 3: Attach the long sides of your frame to the short sides.

... And voilá—you're finished!

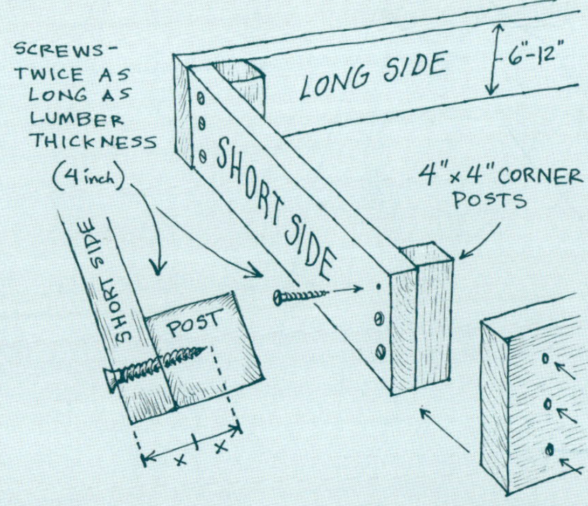

INSTALLATION

When you're done constructing your frame, take it over to its new home. Clear the location of any weeds or debris (you don't need to dig up grass or sod—you can flatten and kill it by using cardboard as a base for the bed). You might want to clear a few feet around the perimeter as well, and fill it in with mulch, pea gravel, or stones to serve as a walkway. Cut your weed barrier to the size of the frame and then lay it down on the bottom. Set the frame on top, and it's ready to fill!

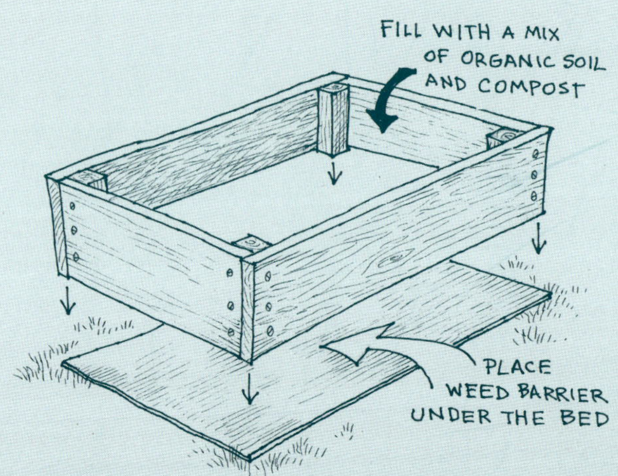

To build a basic wood frame, you'll need four 2 x 6-inch boards, cut to whatever length you prefer. If you want the walls to be higher, you'll work with 8-, 10-, or 12-inch boards. And if you want them to be thicker, that's fine, too. We suggest 2-inch boards as a starting point because they're easy to work with and economical.

Any kind of wood is okay (pine, cedar, etc.), except if it's been "treated." Treated lumber is much of what you'll find at lumber suppliers because it has many commercial uses. Chemicals are applied to the wood to make it fire retardant, slow the natural process of decay, or prevent termites and other insects from inflicting damage. These treatments make the wood more durable for use in the construction of fences, home, and other buildings, but not a good choice for a garden bed. You don't want any of that stuff coming in contact with your soil. So make sure to ask for *untreated* wood.

Additional materials you'll need include corner posts (standard size is 4 x 4-inch), deck screws (twice as long as the lumber thickness to ensure a secure fit — so for a 2-inch board, use 4-inch screws), and a power drill. You'll also need weed cloth (this usually comes in a roll) or another weed barrier such as cardboard to put underneath the wood frame.

Preparing Your Soil

When it comes time to prepare your soil mix, you'll need two ingredients: organic soil and organic compost. You should be able to find these at your local landscape supply company, garden nursery, or big-box hardware store. Any organic garden soil will do. As for compost, try to find one that's a blend of several ingredients (manure, leaf mold, mushrooms, etc.) or buy a few different kinds and mix them together yourself. Good compost should be loose and granular, dark brown in color, and moist but not soggy. If it has a strong unpleasant odor, such as ammonia, then it's immature and shouldn't be used.

To calculate how many cubic feet of soil it will take to fill your raised bed, multiply square footage by height (depth). So a 4' x 4' bed that's one foot tall would need 16 cubic feet of soil (4 x 4 x 1 = 16). A 4' x 4' bed that's ½ foot tall would only need 8 cubic feet (4 x 4 x 0.5 = 8), and so on.

SOIL MATH

TO CALCULATE HOW MUCH SOIL YOU NEED, MULTIPLY L×W×H IN FEET

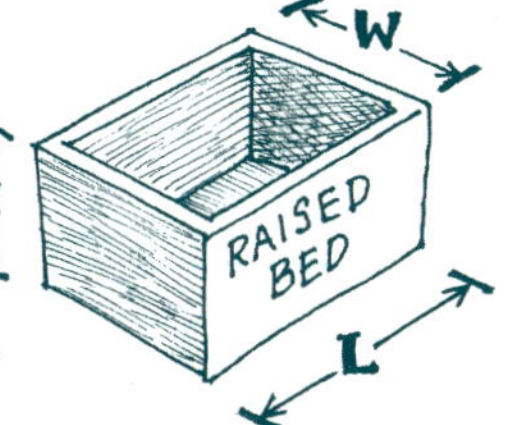

LENGTH × WIDTH × HEIGHT = VOLUME (CUBIC FEET)

MAKING YOUR OWN COMPOST

The practice of composting — that is, having your own dedicated compost enclosure that you add to, maintain, and use throughout the year — can be very rewarding. While homemade compost is the best kind, it takes a good amount of time, space, and dedication to produce. If your interest is piqued and you want to learn more, look ahead to the Beyond the Basics chapter.

Prepare your soil mix by combining equal parts soil and compost. You can use your hands or a garden tool such as a trowel or spade fork. Do your mixing directly in the bed, on a tarp, or in a wheelbarrow. If you don't want to bother with mixing, look for a premixed organic soil that already contains compost. Once you've thoroughly blended the soil and poured it into the bed, sift through it with your fingers, breaking up any chunks and removing twigs or debris. Spread it out until it's level and smooth, taking care not to compact it.

If you're using containers in addition to, or in place of a raised bed, prepare the soil in the same way. A container that's large or deep doesn't need to be filled completely with soil. You can pile shredded newspaper, leaves, rocks, or gravel in the bottom half of the container and fill the top half with your soil mix. Some settling will occur over time, but the container will drain better and you'll end up saving a good amount of soil.

Let's Get Planting!

Finally, it's time to sow your seeds! All cool season crops are incredibly easy to grow from seeds. And nurturing crops for their full life cycle, from seed to harvest, is a magical experience. However, you can start from young plants if you want to reap your rewards a little sooner. We recommend trying at least a few crops from seed (our cool season favorites are peas and leafy greens).

Remember that garden map you made back in March? Now it's time to bring it to life! Review your map and keep it handy while you're planting so you can remember where to put everything.

When you're ready to start, look at the instructions on your seed packet to determine how far apart and how deep to plant your seeds. To calculate seed spacing, you can deviate a bit from the seed packet guidelines, which assume you're planting in rows. Usually you can situate plants a little closer together in a raised bed than you would in rows. So if your seed packet says to plant Swiss chard seeds 6 inches apart, then plant 4 seeds per square foot (and the plants will be 4 inches apart). If the instructions say to space them 4 inches apart, then plant 9 per square foot (and the plants will be 3 inches apart), and so on (look to the "Seed Spacing" table on page 25 for more information).

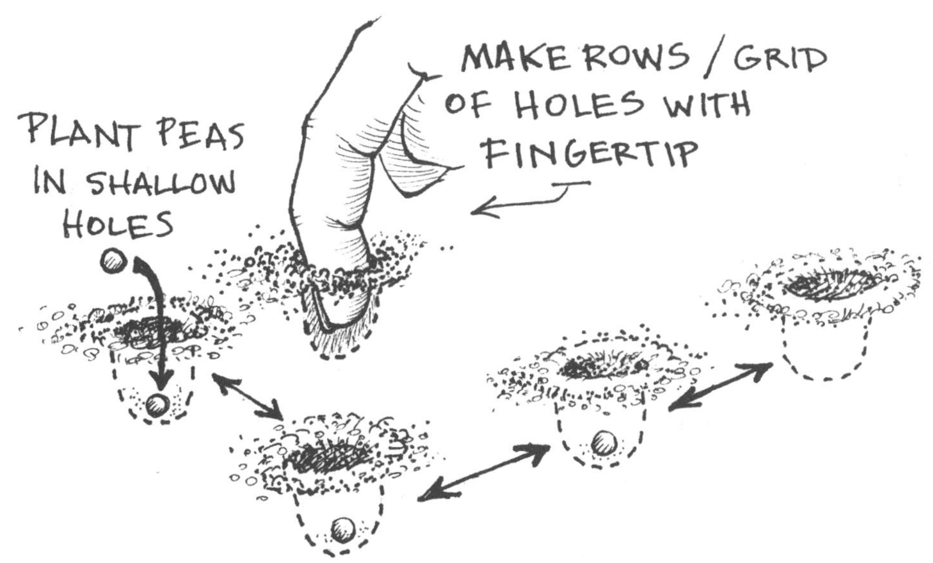

Not all seeds are planted at the same depth. In general, you'll plant 2 – 4 times as deep as the seed's thickness. For large seeds like peas, poke holes in the soil with your finger to the proper depth, insert the seeds, and cover them lightly with soil. Smaller seeds are planted closer to the soil's surface. Take care not to push them in too deep, or they won't germinate.

Seeds for lettuce and other salad greens are quite small, and separating them can be tricky, if not impossible. Go ahead and plant these seeds in small groupings or "pinches" to ensure that at least one germinates. If all of your seeds end up germinating, then you'll see a few seedlings sprouting up in a cluster. Once the seedlings are a couple inches tall, you can "thin" them by removing the extras and leaving the biggest, healthiest looking one intact so that it continues to grow. Trim the extra seedlings at soil level with scissors or garden shears, rather than pulling them by hand, so you don't disturb the roots of the remaining seedling.

Another approach to planting leafy greens (usually not printed on the seed packet) is to "broadcast" or sprinkle the seeds over an area as if you're adding salt to a dish, and then cover them with a very thin layer of soil. Instead of removing extra seedlings, let them continue to grow and harvest their outer leaves every so often for a baby green salad. By cutting only a few leaves at a time from each plant, the plants will stay alive and continue producing. This method of growing is referred to as "cut and come again."

Watering during the germination period is really important. If you're lucky, it rains and nature does the work for you. If not, then you'll need to make sure your soil stays moist in order for the seeds to germinate. This might mean watering every day if the weather is dry. You don't need to soak the soil. Just keep it damp by using a watering can with a rose, a spray bottle that mists, or the fan or mist setting on your hose's spray nozzle (if you use a forceful setting, you might end up washing all the seeds into a corner — oops!)

Continue watering every day after the seeds have sprouted, since they don't have an established root system yet and can dry out quickly. At this point, start watering gently around the base of the seedlings. After the plants have grown an inch or two, you can let them dry out a little between waterings.

All of these watering techniques apply to containers as well. Pay special attention to anything planted in a container, as it will dry out faster than a raised bed. You'll need to water your containers more frequently than your bed — at least once a day, if not more as the weather starts to heat up.

HOW TO READ A SEED PACKET

Seed packets vary in terms of what information they provide and how they depict this information. Details are usually on the back of the packet, but can sometimes be found on the front, too. The seed packet shown here, from Seed Saver's Exchange, is a well-designed and beginner-friendly example.

SEED SAVERS EXCHANGE

④

DIRECT SEED	SEED DEPTH	GERMINATION	THIN
1" Apart	1/4"	5-7 Days	1-6" Apart

③ 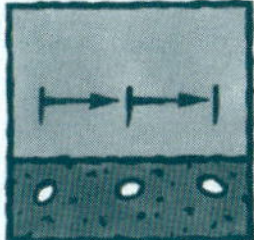 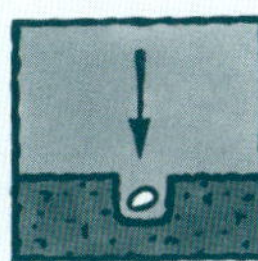  

① **0602A - Arugula** *(Eruca sativa)*

② (aka Roquette or Rocket) Fast-growing cool season salad or sandwich green of Mediterranean origin.
⑦ Sharp distinctive nutty flavor is best when picked young. Self-seeding and hardy. 40-45 days. ⑤

Green Thumb Tip

Sow seeds outdoors as soon as soil can be worked and danger of hard frost has passed. For a continuous supply of arugula, sow every three weeks throughout the summer. Best grown in ⑥ cooler weather. Plant in full sun or partial shade.

Learn More

Find helpful tips on planting and seed saving at www.seedsavers.org/helpfullinks.htm

Photo courtesy of Seed Savers Exchange.

① Plant name (and botanical name)
② Plant description
③ Planting instructions (seed spacing/depth)
④ Days to germination
⑤ Days to maturity
⑥ Light requirements
⑦ Harvest information

You also might find:

- Health information
- Organic certification (if applicable)
- "Packaged for" date (month/year seeds were packaged)
- Seed history (for heirloom varieties)

SEED SPACING

Most seed packets don't list spacing for intensive gardening. This "Seed Spacing" table shows how to convert seed packet math into square foot math.

Spacing recommended on seed packet	12"	8"	6"	4"	3"
How many seeds to plant per square foot	1	2	4	9	16

As your seeds begin to sprout, they can look very similar to one another — especially if you've planted multiple varieties of a certain vegetable ("I think that's leaf lettuce. Wait ... no, it's romaine!"). You'll be able to tell your plants apart when they start to mature and have more defining characteristics. Until then, marking seeds or seedlings when you put them in the ground helps avoid confusion. You can mark seedlings with the plastic inserts that came from the original pots. To mark seeds, you can use tags made from popsicle sticks, paint stirring sticks, cut-up mini-blinds, or terra cotta pot pieces — be creative (this is a fun way to get kids involved). Whatever tags you use, just make sure to label them with a permanent marker so they'll hold up to the weather.

Everything comes to life in April, including weeds. If all of the plants in a square foot area look the same — except for one — chances are it's a weed. With new soil, weeds usually aren't much of an issue. But it's still important to check for them daily and pull them right away while they're young. This will prevent them from getting a foothold and competing with your crops.

STAGGERED PLANTINGS

Believe it or not, there may come a point in the growing season when you have an overabundance of your favorite vegetable. A good way to extend the harvest of a particular veggie and have it available throughout the season, rather than all at one time, is to stagger your plantings. So instead of planting all of your seeds on the same day, sow a group of seeds every week or two, and they'll mature in intervals. Just make sure to plan ahead and reserve space in your raised bed for the plantings.

These are some good crops for staggering:

- Beans ("bush" varieties)
- Beets
- Carrots
- Lettuce
- Peas
- Radishes
- Spinach
- Swiss chard

Protective Devices

Gardening is a labor or love, and it's disheartening when a squirrel digs up your seeds or a rabbit devours your baby lettuce. And while spring crops are good at withstanding cooler temperatures, weather in Chicago can be unpredictable, and some young plants are susceptible to damage from frost and drastic temperature swings. Having some protective devices handy can serve as added insurance against Mother Nature's whims, as well as pesky critters.

One simple device is a floating row cover, which consists of gauze-like material draped directly over plants and secured at the edges with weights. Though made of plastic, row cover material allows sunlight, air, and water to penetrate, and is so lightweight that it seems to "float" on top of plants as they grow. A row cover protects against frost and encourages plant growth by warming the air and soil temperatures by a few degrees. Depending on the temperature, it can be left on your crops throughout the day, or used only at nighttime when temperatures typically dip down. In addition, using a row cover throughout the season can help prevent insects from coming in contact with your plants (more on this in June). Material for row covers typically is sold in a roll and can be reused for several years if handled carefully.

You can also protect individual plants as needed, rather than covering the whole bed at once, with a cloche. Cloches vary in design, but generally are small clear glass or plastic domes that are placed directly over plants. They produce the same effect as a row cover, sealing in warm air and increasing soil temperature. You can buy a cloche or make your own using repurposed household items such as canning jars (turned upside down and removed for part of the day for ventilation) or translucent plastic milk jugs (with the labels, cap, and bottom removed, and anchored into the soil with a straw or small stick). Both cloches and row covers help promote earlier and larger yields of many crops, and they also discourage animals from digging around in your beds.

Like it or not, critters — squirrels, rabbits, birds, skunks, and rats, to name a few — are city dwellers and are here to stay. And for many of you, curious (and beloved!) pets will be equally interested in your new hobby. Diverting these friends will help assure your peace of mind and happy harvest. Cages and fences don't offer a 100% guarantee against intrusion, but they definitely dissuade furry garden thieves. We recommend constructing a cage or fence now while your plants are small, rather than later on in the season. Commonly used materials include hardware cloth, chicken wire, and plastic-coated wire fencing, all of which come in rolls and can be cut to size with pliers and bent into whatever shape you require.

You can make a U-shaped cage that covers the top of your bed, and lift it on and off as needed. This is especially handy for when plants are young and small. As your plants mature, you

Protection from COLD and PESTS

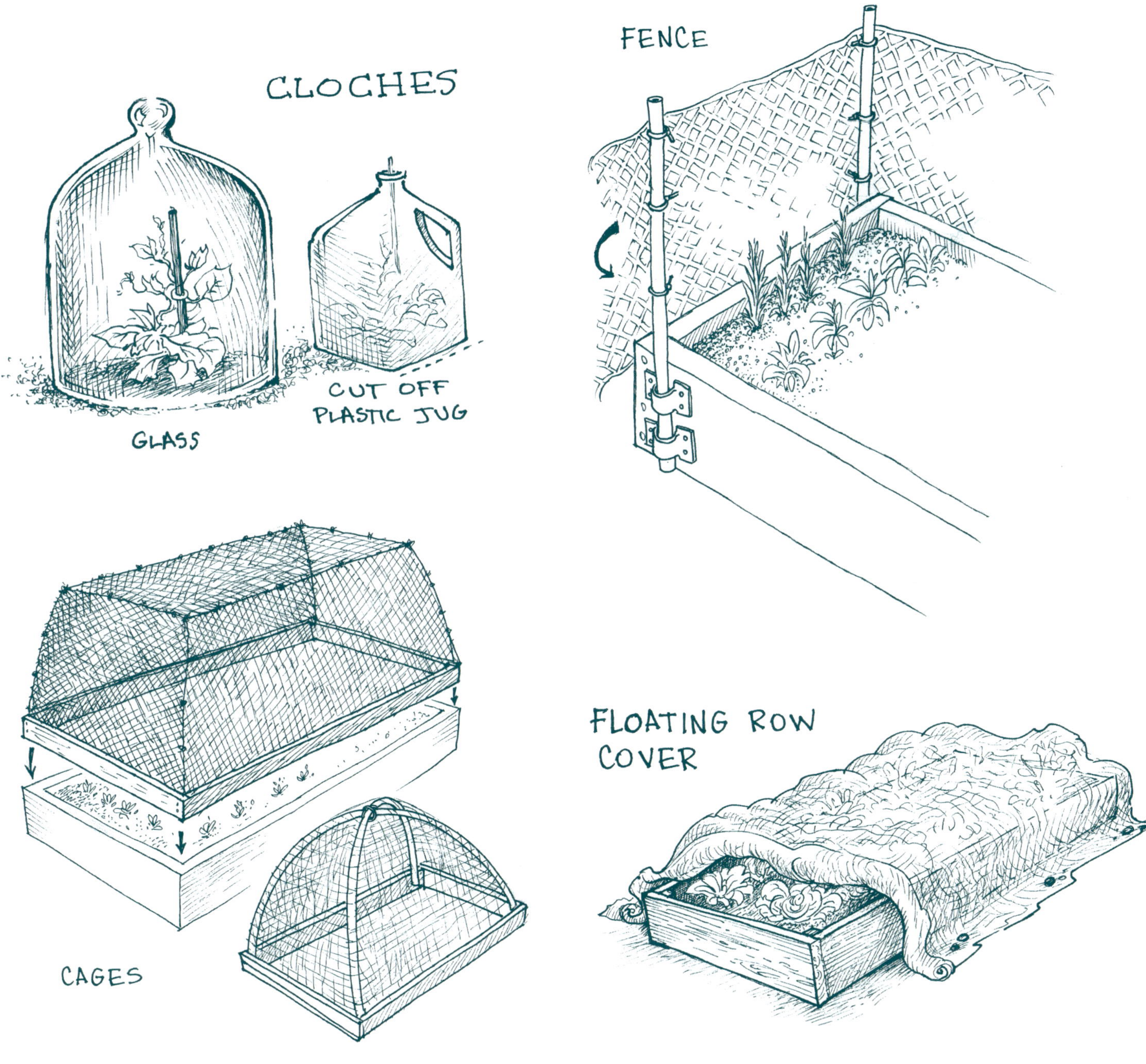

may need to replace the cage with a fence that won't impede upward growth. For added protection against frost or cold temperatures, attach row cover material to the cage with clips or clothespins.

Fences can be built in a couple different ways, depending on whether your bed sits on soil or concrete. If you have soil, then sink metal fence posts into the ground on the outside corners of your bed. For concrete, place PVC pipes on the inside corners of your bed and secure them with U-shaped brackets. Once you've installed your posts or pipes, stretch your fencing material around the perimeter of your bed and attach the ends of the fence with plastic wire ties. Make your fence no more than 3 feet high so you can reach inside the bed comfortably. If you need to guard against the elements, drape row cover material directly over your plants, or stretch it over the top of your fence and secure it with clips or clothespins.

Now ... on to warmer temperatures, more planting, and more growing. The rewards are just beginning!

STARTING FROM SEEDLINGS

If you're starting from a young plant or "seedling" rather than a seed, the transplanting process is pretty straightforward. First make sure your plant is well watered. Dig a hole in your soil the same height as the plant's root ball, and just wide enough to fit the root ball without forcing or squishing it. Then remove the plant from its pot and gently loosen the bottom of the root ball.

You might see some matted roots around the outside of the root ball. This means the plant has become "root-bound" due to the constraints of growing in a pot. Not to worry—you can loosen the roots by "teasing" them out of their circling pattern with your fingers. Tug just the outer roots and leave the core ones intact. It's okay if you hear a little "pop" or "crack" (you're not traumatizing the plant, but encouraging its roots to grow outward). If you aren't able to loosen the roots with your fingers, run a knife along the exterior or bottom of the root ball wherever the matting has occurred.

Now place your seedling into the hole you dug so that it stands straight up, and lightly spread the soil back around it for support. Build a saucer-shaped depression into the soil around the plant's base to help direct water toward the roots. Then water it immediately at the base. The plant may droop at first (a new habitat can be a bit of a shock), but with regular watering, it should perk up within a couple days.

Note: For tomato plants, the transplanting process is a bit different. We'll get to this in May.

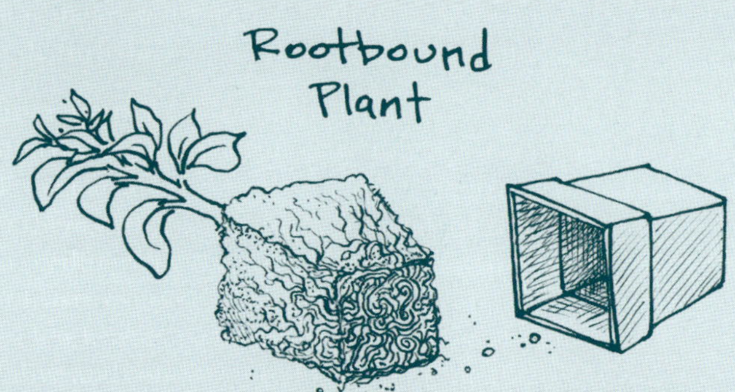

SUPPORT YOUR PEAS

Peas are one of the first crops you can plant in the spring—and they're enthusiastic climbers! You can support them as they grow with a "teepee" shaped trellis that's easy to construct (and a favorite with kids).

Just insert several bamboo poles or stakes (3–5 feet tall) into the soil in a circular pattern around your plants. Then bring the poles together at the top and secure them using garden twine or rope. You won't need to train the peas to grow around the supports. They'll find their way without your help. Enjoy those easy peas!

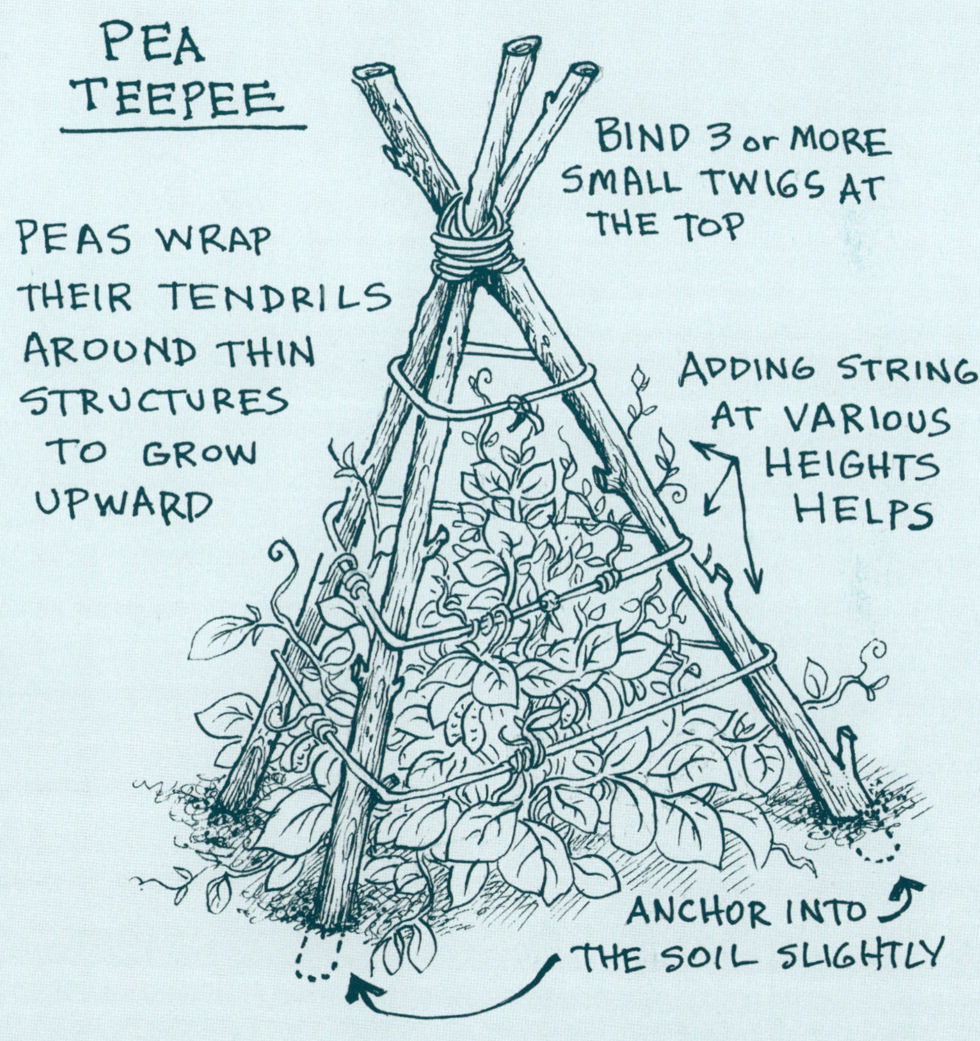

May

May is when your hard work begins to pay off and you can start eating the fruits (and veggies) of your labor. This really is the sweetest reward. In this chapter, we'll offer you some tips on harvesting your cool season crops. And we'll start giving you recipe ideas so you can cook — and share — what you've grown.

In May, the weather's finally stable enough to plant your hot season crops — prized favorites like tomatoes, peppers, and basil, to name a few. We'll advise on what to look for when plant shopping and help demystify some terminology you might encounter. We'll also illustrate some tricks for growing healthy tomatoes, as well as methods for supporting your vertically grown crops.

This is a busy month. Lots to do in the garden... and lots of happiness.

First Harvest

By now your cool season plantings are underway, and some are even ready to harvest. It's the moment you've been waiting for! So pull your peas from the vine, and don't be shy about popping them straight into your mouth. Savoring your first harvest of the season is one of the most deeply connected and blissful moments you'll experience as a food gardener.

It's best to pick your veggies just prior to eating them. This way they'll be at their peak freshness and nutrition. If your schedule doesn't permit this, try to harvest in the early morning or evening when plant stress levels are low. For small root crops such as radishes, carefully pull from the soil by hand. Peas can be harvested by hand as well, with one hand holding the vine and the other gently pinching off the pod (harvest snow peas while the pods are still flat, and sugar snap peas once the pods are plump). Pick peas at least every other day, as frequent picking will help increase yields.

Leaf crops like lettuce or parsley can be snipped with scissors or pinched off by hand. Trim just the outer leaves to promote continued growth of the plant. If you have several varieties, you can take a few leaves from each plant for a mix of flavors. Many greens are sensitive to heat and can wilt quickly after they've been picked, so try not to harvest during peak heat of the day, and be prompt in taking them indoors to cooler temperatures. Greens are best stored unwashed in a plastic bag in your crisper drawer (38° is ideal if you can control the temperature). Put a small paper towel in the bag to absorb extra moisture and help them stay fresh longer. If you have any apples in your fridge, keep them separate from your greens, since apples emit a gas that accelerates the spoiling of greens.

Time to Plant Hot Crops!

As temperatures rise and remain steady, you'll plant your next round of crops. For hot season crops, plant the superstars — tomatoes, peppers, and beans — if nothing else. They're far superior in taste and quality than what you'll buy in the supermarket, and their high yields make them a cost-effective and satisfying choice. It's a luxury to have too many sun-warmed tomatoes (you might use them to bribe your friends for small favors and help in the garden!).

Review seed-to-harvest times (look back to March to find these) when deciding which crops to plant from seeds and which to plant from seedlings. You'll need to allow ample time for plants to mature before the season winds down. Fast-growers like summer squash, beans, and cucumbers can usually be planted from seed. For crops that take longer to mature, like tomatoes, peppers, and eggplant, you're better off starting from seedlings.

Hot season transplants should be latecomers in your garden, as they're highly susceptible to injuries from frost. We suggest planting them no earlier than May 15, or around Mother's Day. In fact, many experienced Chicago gardeners wait until Memorial Day weekend to plant hot crops. Tomatoes, in particular, won't set fruit in temperatures below 58°. So while you might be eager to get them into the ground, it's best to wait until nighttime temperatures are consistently in the mid- to high-50s. They won't grow very fast until then, anyway, so you won't lose much time.

When shopping for seedlings, check for healthy foliage and new growth. Avoid anything that looks diseased or poorly maintained. Often you'll find young plants for sale in four-packs, which are more affordable than a single plant, but a few weeks less mature. A single plant will cost a couple dollars more, but likely will buy you an earlier and longer harvest. If you have no choice but a multi-pack and don't have space for all the plants (one zucchini plant can go a long way in a small garden), give the extras to a neighbor or friend, or consider donating them to a community garden or school gardening program.

Unique Growth Habits

You may see some unfamiliar terminology as you're reading seed and plant labels — specifically for beans, squash, and tomatoes. The terms "bush," "vine," "determinate," and "indeterminate" describe the growth habitat of these plants. Understanding what these terms mean will affect which varieties you buy, where you to choose to locate the plants within your bed, and what devices you use to support them. If the plants aren't labeled with this information, nursery staff should be able to advise you.

To clarify, a "bush" variety is "determinate," meaning that it will grow to a certain size and then stop growing, at which point it will flower and bear all of its fruit within a few weeks. A "vine" variety is "indeterminate," meaning that it will continue growing and producing fruit throughout the entire season, until the first frost. Bush varieties grow lower to the ground (about 3 – 5 feet) and require minimal physical support, while vine varieties can grow quite long (up to 10 or even 15 feet) and need to be trellised in order to thrive and be productive.

You might also run into the term "pole" when shopping for beans. Pole beans are a vine variety, as opposed to bush beans, which are low, self-supporting plants. Situate pole beans near a trellis or other support structure (they look great climbing a chain link fence), and they'll be up and away in no time.

In most cases, winter squash (butternut, acorn, etc.) are indeterminate in their growth habit. Summer squash (zucchini, yellow crookneck, etc.), on the other hand, are usually determinate and have a bush habit. Even so, summer squash plants are not small. In fact, they tend to be space-hoggers and often grow wider than they are tall. But don't let this dissuade you. They can be very prolific, and for many gardeners, they're worth the space they take up.

Growing Vertically

As your vertical crops mature, they'll need support to keep them from sprawling out of control. It's best to install support structures early on while plants are small. If you wait until later, you might disturb their roots. A small cage, trellis, or stakes should be sufficient for most determinate plants. Plants that vine continuously — such as pole beans, winter squash, and melons — will need a taller, wider trellis system. One method is to suspend garden netting between rebar or corner fence posts of your bed.

Your vertical crops will need varying levels of attention throughout the season, depending on their climbing habit. Beans are "self-climbers," so they'll do fine on their own as long as they have a trellis to climb. Cucumbers, winter squash, and melons will wrap their tendrils around nearby supports. You can let them go and they'll find their way, or you can help "train" them to grow in a preferred direction by securing their vines to supports with flexible garden tape, twist ties, or rope (try not to tear the tendrils as you do this — gently unwind them if necessary, and then wrap them back around the supports).

Tomatoes aren't self-climbers, so you'll need to tend to them regularly and train them upward as they grow. Make sure to secure branches to supports before the plants start to bear fruit, as the weight of the fruit can make branches unwieldy and difficult to maneuver.

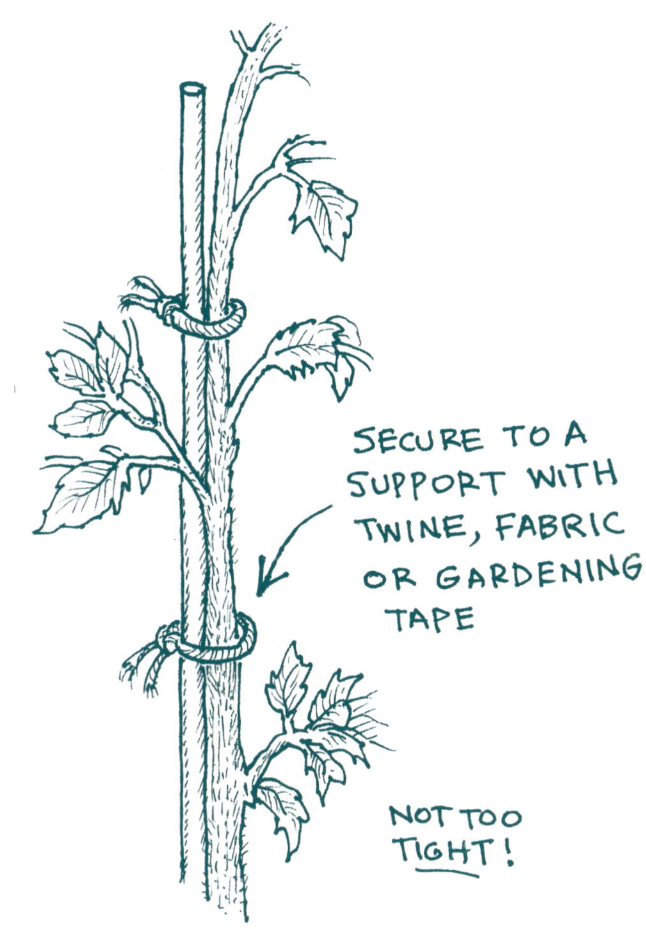

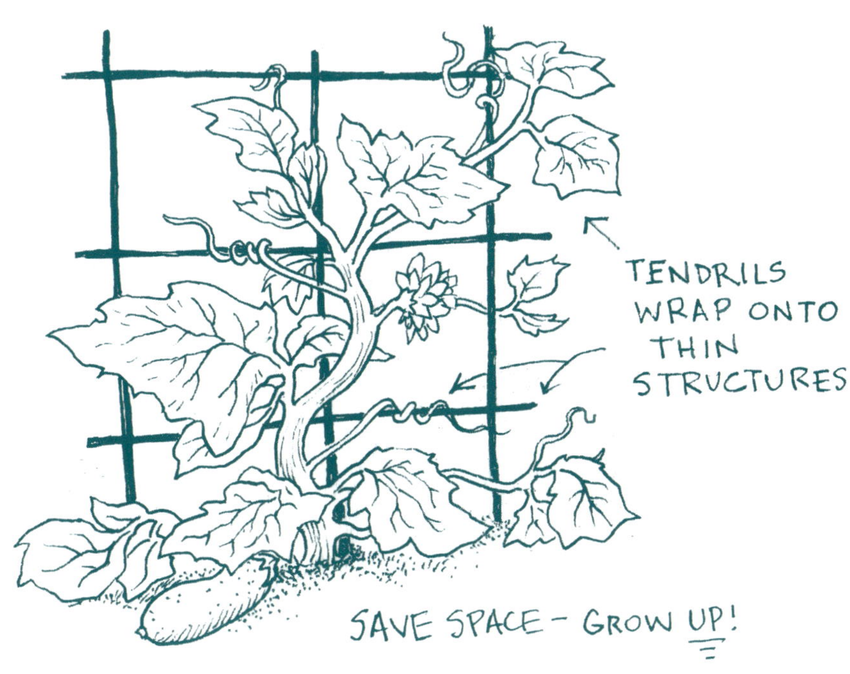

TOMATOES ARE SPECIAL

Tomatoes are by far the most popular home gardening crop. There are hundreds of varieties available, so you'll have no shortage of choices when tomato shopping. Which varieties you select will depend on how you want to use the fruit.

Indeterminate tomatoes are quite versatile and especially good eaten fresh in salads and sandwiches. They can be harvested a few at a time once ripening begins. Their continuous harvest may be preferable if you don't want to deal with lots of tomatoes all at once. Popular types include cherry and beefsteak (you might try starting with one of each).

If you're a tomato junkie, consider planting some determinate varieties as well. They'll require some extra time and commitment, since most of the fruit ripens within two or three weeks and you'll need to harvest and use (or preserve) it all during that time. You can enjoy determinate tomatoes either fresh or cooked. They can't be beat for making large batches of sauce, salsa, or paste. In fact, they're often called "paste" tomatoes. They're also well suited for canning and dehydrating. You can spread your harvest throughout the season by choosing varieties with different maturity dates and staggering planting times.

"Heirloom" tomatoes have become increasingly popular in recent years — and for good reason. They taste much better than what you buy at the supermarket. Commercially grown tomatoes are bred to maintain a long shelf life and withstand shipping, often at the expense of flavor. Heirloom varieties also offer distinct colors and shapes — beyond the typical red and round — that you won't readily find outside of home gardens. Growing heirloom fruits and veggies is a time-honored home gardening tradition (to learn more about heirloom seeds and plants, see "The Truth About Seeds" in January/February).

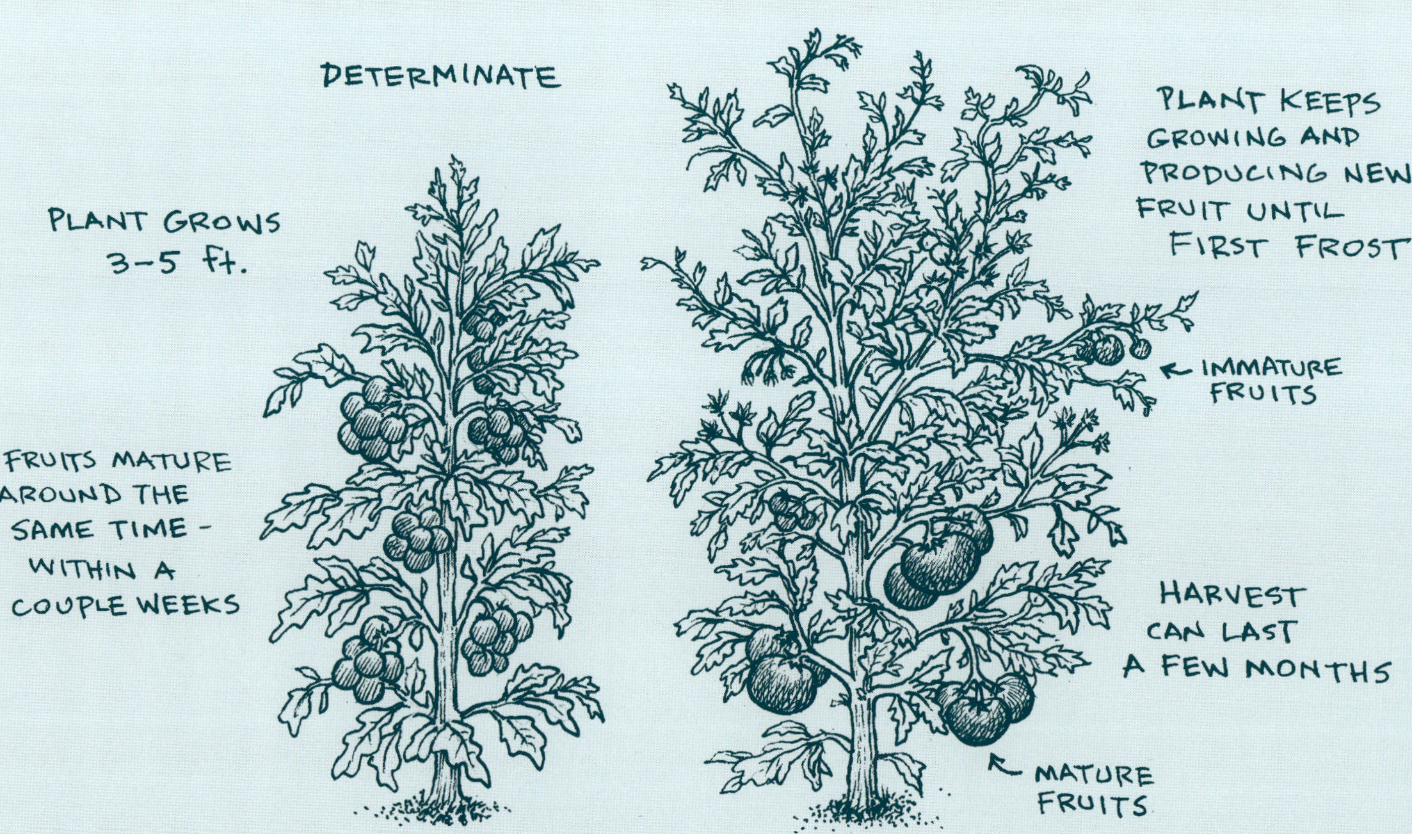

HEIRLOOM FAVORITES

Here's a short list of heirloom tomatoes that grow well in the Chicago area, divided according to how they're best used.

Slicing

- Brandywine
- Dr. Wyche's Yellow
- Earliana
- German Pink
- Green Zebra
- Jaunne Flamme (orange)
- Moonglow (yellow)
- Paul Robeson (purple)
- Pink Oxheart
- Purple Cherokee
- Sheboygan
- Silver Fir Tree
- Tasty Evergreen

Salad

- Austin's Red Pear
- Black Cherry
- Blondkopfchen
- Currant Sweet Pea
- White Cherry

Sauce

- Amish Paste
- Italian Gold
- Plum Lemon (yellow)
- Rosso Sicilian
- San Marzano
- Striped Roman

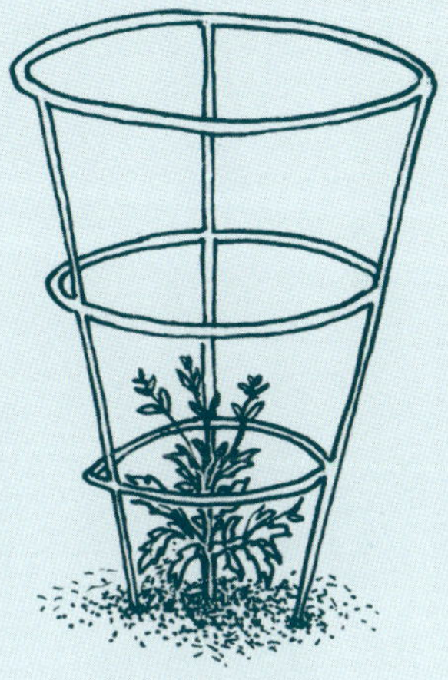

SUPPORT STRUCTURES

Regardless of what tomato varieties you choose, your plants will need some form of physical support as they grow. Tomato support structures, commonly referred to as "cages," come in many styles including square, round, cone, and ladder-shaped. They cost anywhere from $1–10. Flimsy cages that look like they're made of coat hanger wire won't provide adequate support, so don't bother with these. Look for cages that are tall and made of heavy gauge wire, with multiple long anchor points that will extend securely into the soil. These may cost a few dollars more, but are worth the investment.

For determinate tomatoes, a 4 or 5-foot cage is usually sufficient. If you're using a cone-shaped cage, we recommend adding a stake to the plant as well. This will help keep the plant growing upright, and the cage will be less likely to tip over. Use a tall, heavy piece of wood or metal for your stake. Insert it into the soil about 2 inches away from the plant's stem, and secure it to the stem periodically as the plant grows.

Indeterminate tomatoes will require heavy-duty support. They grow all season long and can produce vines from 6 to 10 feet in length, depending on the variety. That's a lot of foliage and a lot of weight, especially once fruit production starts. So plan accordingly. If your raised bed is situated near a wall, fence, or other vertical structure, you can secure your tomato cages to any of these structures for added support. You can also attach the cages to corner fence posts in your bed. Anything helps!

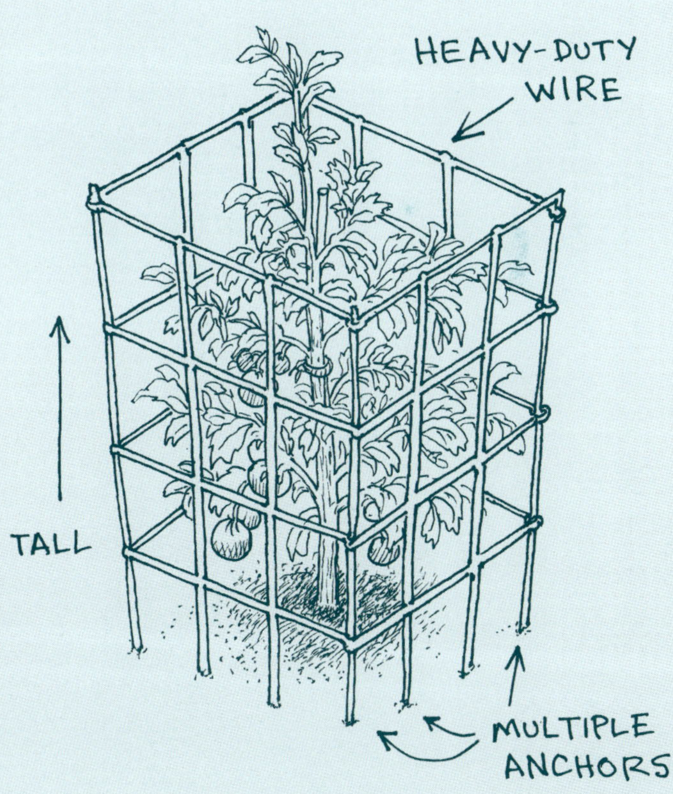

HOW TO PLANT TOMATOES

What's the secret to growing great tomatoes? There's no simple answer, but we think a good place to start is in the roots. With a strong root system, tomato plants need less water and can better withstand summer storms—and they're likely to yield more fruit.

You can encourage root development by planting tomatoes differently than you would other seedlings. Tomatoes can develop roots all along their stems, so burying a large portion of the stem when you put it in the ground will increase the size of the root system.

First dig a shallow trench as long as your seedling is tall. Trim off the leaves from the lower portion of the stem (this is the part that you'll bury). Remove the seedling from its pot and loosen the root ball a bit, then lay it horizontally into the trench. Fill the trench with soil and gently bend the stem upward (don't worry—it will straighten up as it grows). Give the plant water right away after planting to avoid transplant shock, and then water it daily for the first week or so until it's settled into its new home.

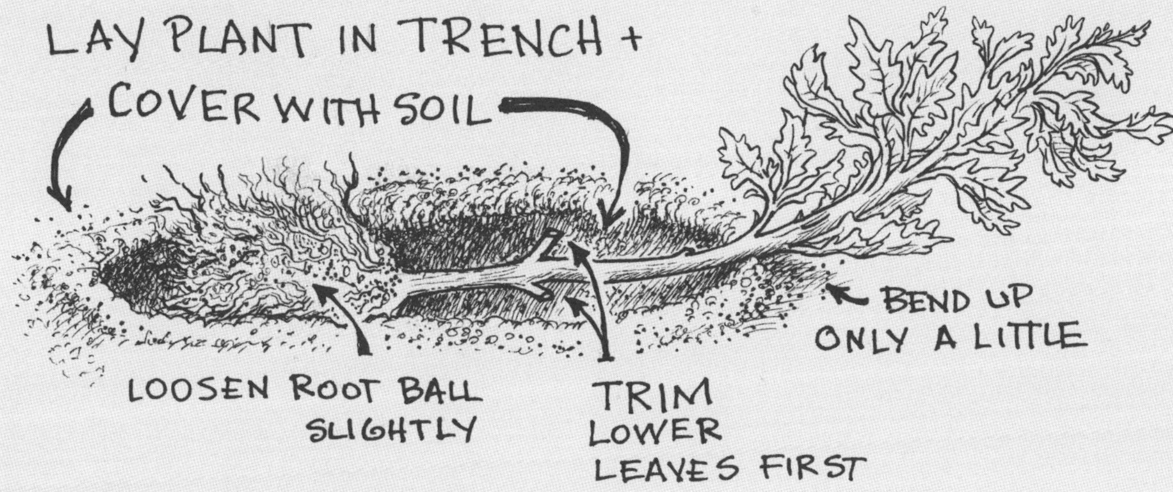

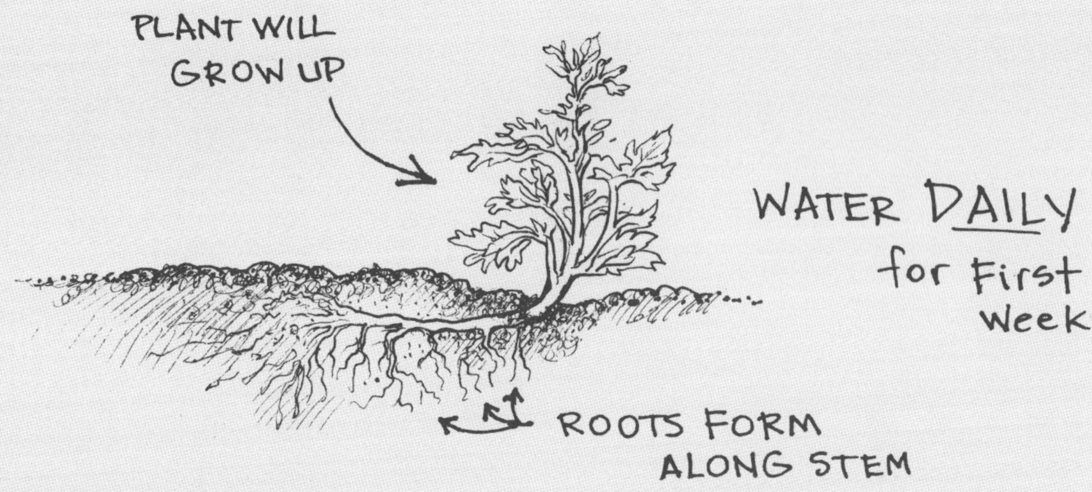

Watering Dos and Don'ts

Overhead watering methods like sprinklers are fine for lawns and shrubs, but not for vegetables. Excessive moisture on leaves can harbor fungal diseases, and if an infected plant is watered from above or the side, the disease can spread to other nearby plants. Your plants need water sent to their roots. The best way to do this is by hand watering or positioning your hose nozzle close to the base of your plant.

We know that water play is a mainstay of summer fun. We're not down on playing with the hose or sprinklers. Just point them in a direction other than your garden, and tell the kids to squirt each other instead of the vegetables. If your kids want to water the garden, show them how (and enjoy the help!).

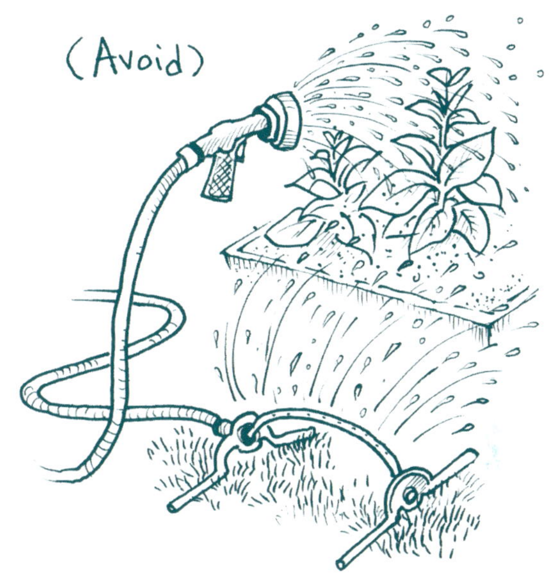

Garden Journal

Toward the end of May, you'll finally have everything planted and be done digging in the soil (for a little while, at least). Take a few moments to rest, sit back, and admire what you've accomplished so far.

In your down time, consider starting a garden journal. By recording your observations throughout the season, you can keep track of what you've learned and plan better for next year's garden. You might jot down planting dates, the amount harvested and when it was ready, which crops thrived and which fared poorly, which tastes you liked best and which things never to plant again, sun patterns throughout the season, insect problems, diseases ... the list goes on. In addition to written notes, you can convey visual information with a garden map, drawings, and photographs. We're the first to admit — it's easy to be lazy about journaling. But if you do adopt this habit, you'll be a better gardener for it.

RECIPE BOX

Fettuccine with Greens

First harvest of the season means lots of green. This recipe doesn't skimp on the leafy herbs. Mix them with asparagus and spinach fettuccine for some extra green goodness!

Ingredients

1 pound spinach fettuccine (or substitute plain)

1 large bunch asparagus, woody ends trimmed off, remaining tender parts cut into 2-inch pieces

3 large garlic cloves, minced

1 cup flat leaf parsley, coarsely chopped

¼ cup chives, finely chopped

3 cups arugula leaves

Olive oil

Salt and freshly ground black pepper

Shredded Parmesan cheese

Instructions

In a large pot, bring 6 quarts of water to a rolling boil. While you're waiting for the water to boil, heat 1–2 tablespoons of olive oil in a large skillet over medium heat. Add asparagus and cover; cook for 4–5 minutes until tender, but still bright green, turning several times (thin spears will cook more quickly than thick ones). Add garlic and a dash of salt and pepper, and sauté uncovered for another minute or so until garlic turns golden. Turn heat to low and add greens; cook for 1–2 more minutes, stirring often, until greens are wilted. Set aside.

Add pasta and 3 tablespoons of salt to boiling water. Stir occasionally to prevent pasta from sticking. Cook until tender but firm to the bite (pasta package should indicate cooking time). Drain thoroughly.

Combine pasta and greens. Drizzle in a little more olive oil and add salt and pepper to taste. Toss until mixed. Top with Parmesan cheese just before serving.

Serves 6.

Sugar Snap Peas with Edamame Hummus

Nothing compares to the sweet crunch of a sugar snap pea. Our favorite way to enjoy them is raw—plain and simple. But you can pair them with hummus dip for a little something extra. This recipe calls for edamame (young soybeans) in place of the traditional chickpea. Serve this dish again later in the season with bell peppers, cucumbers, or other "dipping" veggies you have on hand.

Ingredients

1 cup cooked edamame

¼ cup tahini (sesame seed paste)

4 tablespoons lemon juice (about 1 lemon)

1 garlic clove, peeled

¼ teaspoon salt

4 tablespoons olive oil

Sugar snap peas for dipping

Instructions

Wash peas and pat dry. Remove fibrous strings that run the length of the pods; break off the stems and pull downward, and the strings should come right off. Or use a knife to cut off the tips of the pods, then pull downward to remove the strings. Set peas aside.

Combine edamame, tahini, lemon juice, garlic, and salt in a food processor or blender. Process until smooth. Add olive oil and continue to process until oil is fully incorporated. Serve in a dipping bowl alongside peas (and other raw veggies, if you like).

Makes about 1¼ cups of hummus.

June

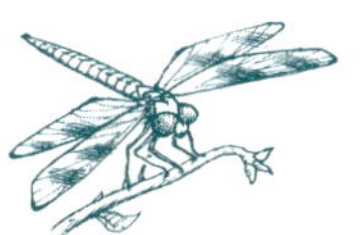

By June, things are getting pretty tasty. Your harvest is steadily increasing and you're spending more time in the kitchen. You might notice that growing your own food is changing the way you cook, and you're planning your menus around the produce that you have on hand. Yes, you might end up eating zucchini for a month, but figuring out how to cook it 10 different ways is part of the fun!

After May's hustle to plant and get the garden in order, June can seem calm, if not routine. Your hot crops are in the ground and your cool ones are dwindling. You water and weed. You spend a lot of time staring at your tomatoes, wishing they would grow faster. June is a time to tend and observe. It's also the month when you might detect insects and disease starting to appear on your plants. But don't panic. We'll help you treat these conditions organically and offer ways to help prevent them from occurring again.

Keep Your Cool Crops Going

Your cool crops are nearing the end of their course by now. Maybe you're done with lettuce and want to move on. Or maybe you can't get enough of it! If this is the case, try your hand at growing cool crops through the summer. You can make additional sowings or work on extending your current crops for a few more weeks. The trick is protecting sensitive varieties from the heat.

As days get longer and temperatures rise, cool crops can "bolt," or enter a rapid growth phase as they attempt to flower and produce seeds. All plants "go to seed" eventually. This is how they reproduce and preserve their species. You'll know your plant has bolted if its stem is long and spindly, its leaves are few, and it starts to produce a flower (in particular, you can tell lettuce has bolted when you pick a leaf and an opaque white substance oozes out). Once a plant sends energy toward producing a flower instead of leaves, its flavor can become bitter. Crops that are prone to bolting are leafy greens, basil, celery, broccoli, and cauliflower.

For most herbs and vegetables, the bolting phase is a sign of being done — at least as far as eating is concerned. But for a few varieties, this isn't the case. Some seeds are edible and as delicious as their parent plants were prior to bolting. Dill seeds are a familiar ingredient in Swedish cooking and pickle-making, and cilantro seeds, also known as coriander, are popular in Indian cuisine. Basil flowers are lovely to look at (some varieties of basil are grown just for their flowers), but if you're diligent about pinching back the blossoms, the leaves of the plant will remain tasty for a long time. Spicy greens like arugula just get spicier as they start to produce flowers. Let your taste buds be the judge of whether your plant's time is up.

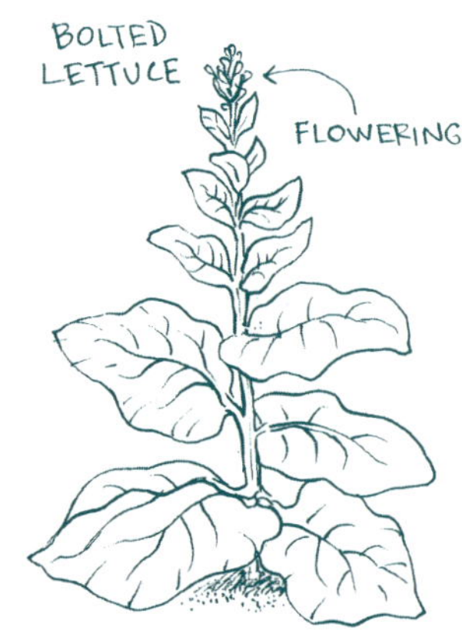

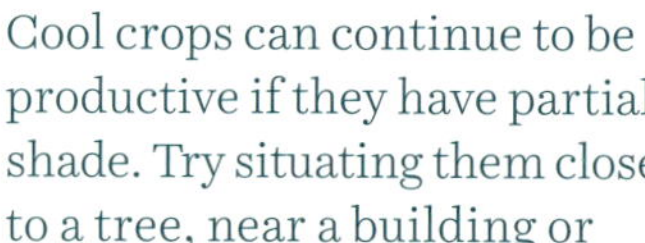

Cool crops can continue to be productive if they have partial shade. Try situating them close to a tree, near a building or structure that casts a shadow, or to the north of a vertical crop such as tomatoes or beans. Another effective method is to cover the plants with a shade cloth throughout the day or during peak heat of the day (mid- to late afternoon). Shade cloth is made of knitted polyethylene fabric and is rated by the percentage of sunlight that it blocks (40–50% is usually sufficient). It can be cut to size, stretched over your bed, and secured to fencing or other supports with clips or clothespins. The material is durable and can last up to 10 years with proper care.

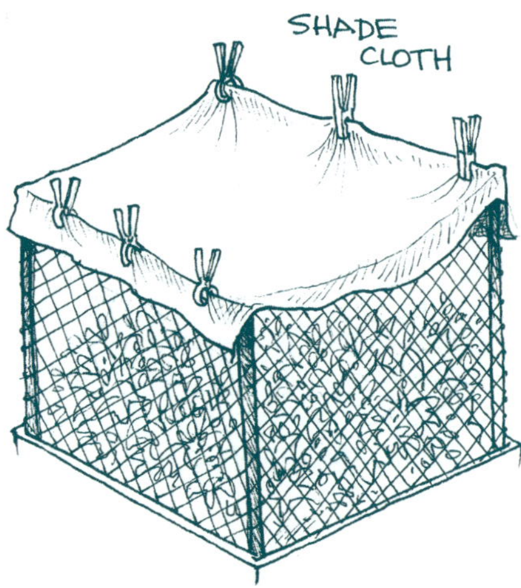

Harvest Hints

June yields are largely dependent on the weather, and temperatures in Chicago are famously variable from one year to the next and from one area to another. The expression "cooler by the lake" often rings true during the summer. If it's a cool June, then your heat-loving veggies will take their time ripening.

Beans and cherry tomatoes are some of the first hot crops to mature. You'll see them start to appear toward the end of the month. Since they're small, they can easily be pulled from the vine by hand (and eaten right away for a taste of heaven!). Harvest beans before their pods start to bulge, and at least every other day to encourage production. Cherry tomatoes can crack if left on the vine too long, so pick them promptly once they look ripe.

Keep an eye on your larger tomatoes as well. You'll see them gradually change from green to red (or yellow, or orange, depending on the variety). Be patient for now. They'll start to fully mature in July.

Favorites like cucumbers, zucchini, and hot peppers might be ready for harvest in late June. These don't always pull easily by hand from their strong weight-bearing stems. It's best to use scissors or shears to snip them from the vine, rather than twisting or yanking them off, which risks tearing the fruit or stem of the plant. Cucumbers and zucchini, in particular, grow very quickly. Pick them while they're small (6–8 inches long) for better flavor. Harvest hot peppers as needed (larger peppers like bells and poblanos will ripen later in the summer).

To harvest your long-awaited broccoli or cauliflower, cut off the central head while it's still firm and tight, before it starts to loosen and separate. If you leave the rest of the plant intact, it often will form side shoots with bite-sized heads for a few more weeks. You can do the same thing with cabbage. Harvest the main head but not the outer leaves, and small heads will develop along the leaf axis.

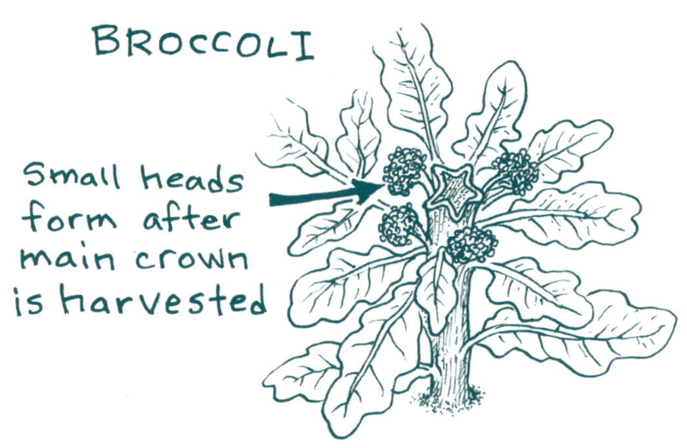

Daily Maintenance

At this point in the season, daily maintenance tasks — garden "hygiene," as we like to call it — take up the biggest chunk of your gardening time. While these tasks might seem mundane, they're vital to the health and productivity to your garden.

Most importantly, water your plants on a regular basis. How often depends on the weather and soil conditions. If the foliage on your plants is wilting or drooping, the plants probably need a drink. Also, if you stick your finger a few inches down into the soil and it's dry, you need to water. It's best to water in early morning or at night to minimize evaporation. Remember to water at the stem and around the base of plants, and avoid getting the foliage too wet, as prolonged moisture on leaves can lead to fungal and bacterial growth. On really hot days, even well watered plants can still droop. Don't worry — they should perk up once the sun goes down.

Keep scouting for weeds, and pull or cut them off early before they go to seed and begin to spread. Consider adding a layer of mulch on top of your soil to help keep weeds at bay. Mulch also can help regulate soil temperature and conserve moisture, so you won't need to water as often. You can purchase mulch or use your own garden "waste" materials such as dry leaves, grass clippings, straw, or fine wood chips. Make sure that whatever material you use is organic (packaging on a store-bought kind should indicate whether it's organic), and avoid mulch that has been colored or treated with chemicals, since the colorants and chemicals will break down and absorb into your soil over time. Mulching is a matter of personal preference. Some gardeners swear by it, while others don't bother.

"Do I need to fertilize?" you might be wondering. The answer is, probably not. Your soil should be plenty healthy this first season, since it's fresh and new. Soil "amendments" might be necessary in seasons to come (to learn more, see our Beyond the Basics chapter). If you're in doubt, you can always add a thin layer of compost to the top of your soil.

For fruiting plants, in particular — like tomatoes, peppers, and eggplants — you have the option of fertilizing when blossoms first appear. Choose an organic granular fertilizer that's high in phosphorus to help support fruit production. Using about ¼ cup of fertilizer per plant, "side-dress" each plant by sprinkling the fertilizer in a circle around the base, 3 inches away from the stem to avoid "burning" the plant (the nitrogen in fertilizer can sometimes cause this reaction). The fertilizer will be absorbed into the soil as you water your plants.

Pest and Disease Management

Now is the time to start inspecting your garden for signs of pests or disease. Chances are you won't encounter many, since your garden is new and your soil is fresh and healthy. If you do, it's not cause for alarm. Just resist the urge to reach for a can of bug spray.

There are a variety of organic ways to manage pests and disease. Commonly used preventive methods include proper watering, providing air circulation to plants (by trellising and pruning), using protective barriers (such as floating row covers), eliminating habitats where pests and disease can proliferate, removing diseased material before it spreads, and crop rotation (more on this in the Beyond the Basics chapter). You can also plant specific herbs and flowers alongside your vegetable crops to discourage certain pests and attract beneficial insects. These herbs and flowers do this naturally through their organic chemical make-up.

"Beneficial insects?" you ask. Yes, there are such things! Not all insects are bad. In fact, many bugs improve the health of your garden ecosystem. Pollinators like bees and wasps help your plants produce fruit, and ground-dwelling beetles and worms enrich the soil. Predatory insects control unwanted pests by feeding on them. For example, ladybugs and lacewings have a healthy appetite for aphids.

How can you tell when an insect is bad? If it's causing damage to your plant in any way, consider it a pest. In many cases, pest insects are short-lived and don't require any action. Otherwise, the best way to control pests is to remove them by hand and either squish them or drown them in a bucket of soapy water. You can also prune affected leaves and fruit and throw them in the garbage. And while we did tell you awhile back not to hose down your plants, in the event of an infestation, you're allowed to spray affected leaves and wash the unwanted visitors away. As a last resort, use the least toxic chemical controls you can find, such as homemade soap spray, horticultural oils, or botanicals (but remember, these may kill the good bugs as well as the bad).

If you have pests in your garden, it doesn't mean you're a bad gardener. Similarly, if your plants show signs of disease, don't blame yourself. Plant diseases are often the result of weather conditions, and their onset is usually beyond your control. Diseases are rarely fatal to plants, but can spread quickly, so it's important to catch them early on. Removal of affected plant parts is often enough to control the spread of infection.

Okay... enough about disease and pests. If you encounter problems that you can't identify or successfully treat, contact your county extension service agent, whose trained horticultural experts can assist you (see the Resources section for more information).

BENEFICIAL INSECTS

Here are some good bugs to look out for. If you see any of these crawling or buzzing around, leave them be and they'll do their work.

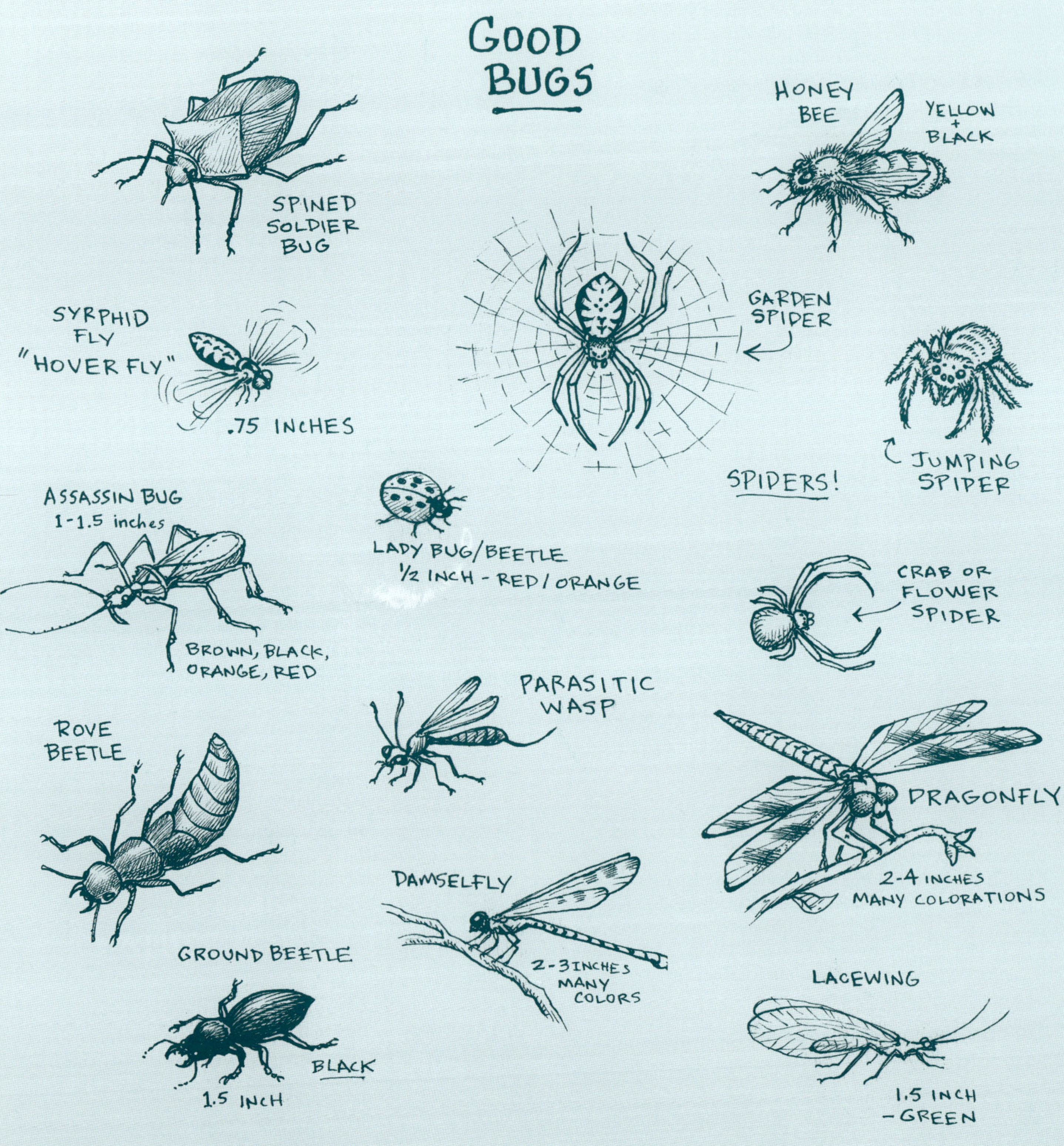

PLANTS THAT ATTRACT BENEFICIAL INSECTS

Plant	Attracts
Angelica	Lacewings, lady beetles, parasitic wasps
Anise	Lady beetles, parasitic wasps, tachinid flies
Asteraceae family (asters, daisies, sunflowers)	Bees, hoverflies, lacewings, lady beetles, parasitic wasps, tachinid flies
Dill	Bees, hoverflies, lady beetles, spiders, wasps
Lovage	Beneficial wasps, (shelters) ground beetles
Marigold	Hoverflies, parasitic wasps
Nasturtium	(Shelters) ground beetles and spiders
Zinnia	Bees, lady beetles, parasitic flies, parasitic wasps

PLANTS THAT DISCOURAGE PESTS

Plant	Discourages
Anise	Aphid
Catnip	Aphid, cabbage looper, cabbage worm, cucumber beetle, flea beetle, squash bug
Chives	Aphid
Coriander	Aphid, carrot fly
Dill	Cabbage looper, cabbage worm, tomato hornworm
Fennel	Aphid, slug, snail
Feverfew	Aphid
Geranium	Cabbage worm, corn earworm, leafhopper, Japanese beetle
Lavender	Aphid
Marigold	Mexican bean beetle, nematode, whitefly
Nasturtium	Aphid, cabbage looper, cabbage worm, cucumber beetle, squash bug, whitefly
Peppermint	Ant, aphid, cabbage looper
Petunia	Aphid, leafhopper, Mexican bean beetle, squash bug
Rosemary	Cabbage looper, cabbage maggot, carrot fly, Mexican bean beetle
Sage	Cabbage looper, cabbage maggot, cabbage worm, carrot fly
Spearmint	Ant, aphid, cabbage looper, flea beetle, squash bug
Thyme	Cabbage looper, cabbage worm, whitefly

COMMON PESTS

Don't let this section freak you out. It's just a list of pests that you might encounter, and how to recognize and manage them if need be. They won't all show up in your garden, and they can be managed with a bit of vigilance.

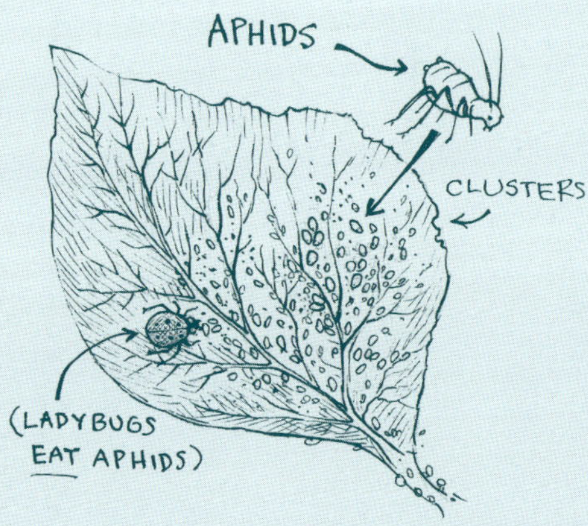

Aphids

Aphids are small, sucking insects that eat the soft tissue in plants—particularly new growth. Look for them in the head of the plant or on the underside of leaves. They're about one tenth of an inch long and green, black, brown, or gray in color. Aphids rarely cause severe damage to plants, but they do reproduce quickly, so eliminate them early if you can.

Organic Antidote: Wash off with a heavy stream of water or homemade soap spray (dissolve one tablespoon of dish soap into three cups of water).

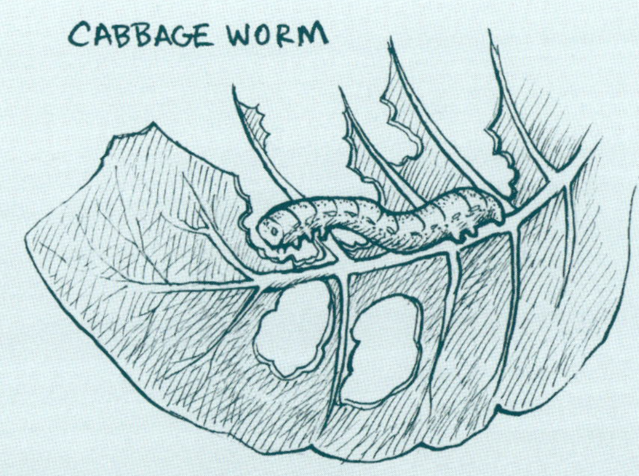

Cabbage Worms and Loopers

A cabbage worm is the larva of a butterfly, and a cabbage looper is the larva of a moth. Both like to munch on the Brassica family of plants (cabbage, broccoli, etc.), as well as leafy greens. Look for holes in leaves or leaves that have been reduced, at least in part, to their spines. The caterpillars have hearty appetites, so try to catch them while they're small. At full size, they're about an inch and a half long. The caterpillars can be difficult to see since they're green and blend in with the plants. Check the underside of leaves or in the head of the plant for piles of moist, dark green frass (poop).

Organic Antidote: Lure caterpillars off the plant with a stiff wire or stick. Then snip them with scissors or drop them into a pail of soapy water. Use a floating row cover to help prevent them from coming into contact with plants.

Cucumber Beetle

Cucumber beetles primarily affect cucumbers, squash, and melons. There are two kinds: striped, which has a yellow body and three black stripes; and spotted, which is yellow with twelve black spots on its back. Both are about a quarter of an inch long. Signs of infestation include chewed leaves and stems, and marks on fruit. The beetles also spread bacteria on the plants when they munch on them, causing leaves to wilt.

Organic Antidote: Hand-pick and squish beetles, and prune off and destroy any plant parts that show signs of bacterial wilt. You can protect seedlings with a floating row cover.

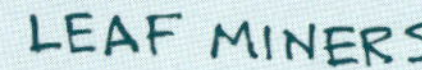

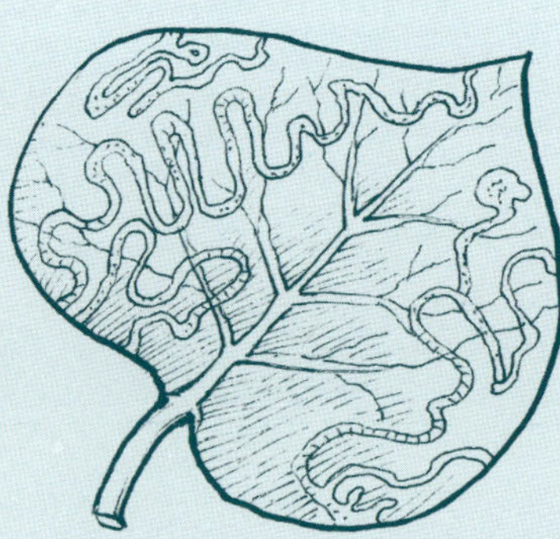

Leaf Miners

Leaf miners are larvae of small flies that live in and eat the inner membrane of plant leaves. You'll see the damage before you see the insect itself. Look for dried brown patches or maze-like patterns on leaves.

Organic Antidote: Remove affected leaves, since it's hard to reach the insects inside the leaves. Floating row covers help prevent flies from laying their eggs in the first place.

Slugs and Snails

Slugs and snails eat all kinds of vegetation, including leaves, stems, and the fruit of plants. If you see large chunks missing from your plants, chances are a snail or slug is nearby. During the day they retreat to damp, shady spots. Look under big rocks, piles of grass clippings, or other debris-laden areas to find them. It's best to do this at dusk, at night with a flashlight, or on a rainy day.

Organic Antidote: Remove by hand, and eliminate their habitats as well (this includes staking up any large veggies that are resting on the soil). Repel them by putting a copper barrier around your bed (the flexible "tape" emits a natural electrical charge), or use non-toxic baits such as iron phosphate or beer (poured into a pie tin and sunk into the soil).

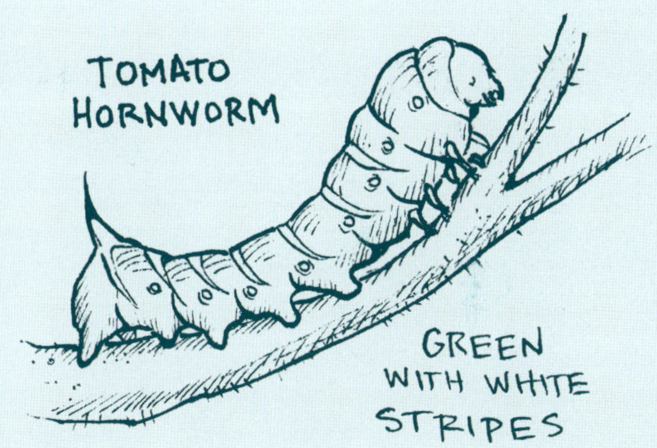

Squash Vine Borer

Squash vine borers prefer winter squash, zucchini and other summer squash, and to a lesser degree, melon plants. The borers are larvae of moths that lay their eggs at the plant's base. Caterpillars develop and feed inside the stalk, migrating to the main stem. If you catch the larvae early, you can effectively control them. Check for dots of frass protruding from holes on the stem of the plant, near the base. If you see wilting vines or leaves, it may be too late to save the plant.

Organic Antidote: Use a knife to carefully cut the stem along its axis where you see signs of infestation. Split open the stem and look for the caterpillar—it will be cream colored and up to an inch long. Remove it with a toothpick or stiff wire, then squish it or snip it in half. Cover the hole in the stem immediately with moist soil. You can prevent egg-laying by wrapping the lower stem of the plant in nylon stockings or aluminum foil, or by using a floating row cover (until the plant starts blooming, at which point it will need to stay uncovered so it can pollinate).

Tomato Hornworm

Tomato hornworms are the larvae of hawk or sphinx moths and commonly affect tomatoes, as well as eggplants, peppers, and potatoes. The caterpillar is green in color with eight white V-shaped marks along its sides and a black "horn" projecting from its rear end. At full size, it's three to four inches long. Even though hornworms are quite large, they blend well into plant foliage, so you'll probably notice damage to plants before you see the caterpillars themselves. Look for stripped leaves and piles of black frass on and around the plants.

Organic Antidote: Since they're so big, hornworms are easy to remove by hand. You can squish them, snip them with scissors, or toss them into a pail of soapy water.

COMMON DISEASES

Here are a few common diseases that you might see at this point in the season, their symptoms, and methods for treating them.

Plant diseases often are contagious. When you're done working on infected plants, make sure to wash your hands and disinfect your gardening tools to help prevent the spread of disease (skip ahead to November/December for tips).

Blossom End Rot

Blossom end rot can affect tomatoes, peppers, squash, and other fruiting vegetables. It's caused by a calcium deficiency in the fruit and often occurs due to erratic weather as the fruit begins to set (if the plant gets too dry or too wet, its ability to absorb calcium from the soil is diminished). Blossom end rot is most often seen on the first fruit of the season as dark brown, leathery, sunken spots on the blossom, or bottom, end of the fruit.

Organic Antidote: Pick and discard damaged fruit in the trash (and rest assured this isn't a life sentence for your plant—subsequent fruit probably will turn out just fine). Help prevent onset by watering attentively and trying to maintain a consistent moisture level in your soil. You might try adding a layer of mulch. Watering deeply a couple times a week is more effective than watering superficially every day.

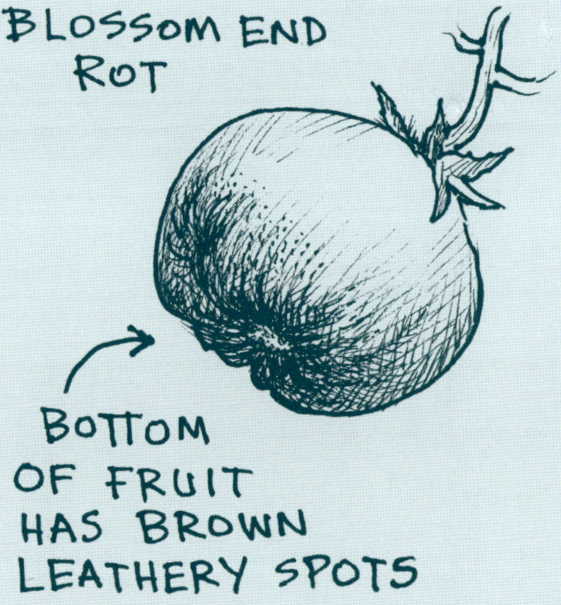

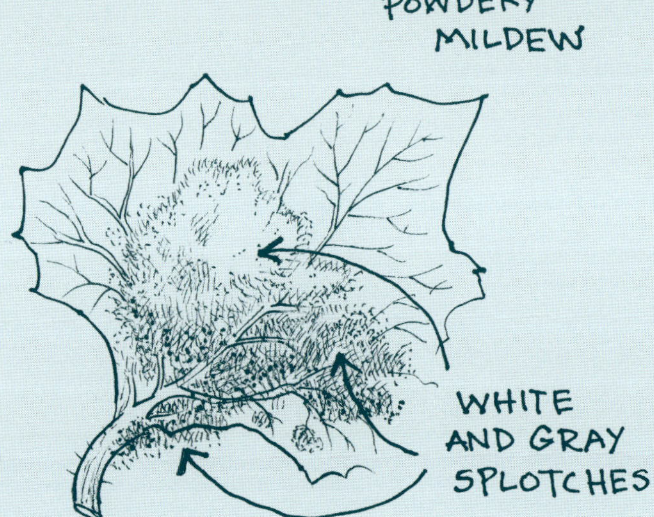

Powdery Mildew

Powdery mildew is a fungal disease that favors squash, cucumbers, and melons. It's usually caused by conditions of high humidity, crowded plantings, or poor air circulation. You'll recognize it as powdery splotches of white or gray, most often on the top surfaces of leaves and stems of plants, and at times on lower leaf surfaces, flowers, buds, and fruit. Powdery mildew isn't fatal, but if enough of the plant is covered, it can become stressed and fruit quality can diminish.

Organic Antidote: Trim off any infected plant parts and discard them in the trash. Improve air circulation by thinning and pruning as appropriate, and make sure to water under foliage, not on top of it. To help prevent the onset of powdery mildew, apply weekly sprayings of baking soda solution (one teaspoon of baking soda dissolved into one quart of water) to susceptible plants during humid weather.

Tomato Blight

Many tomato diseases are lumped into the category of "blight": early blight, late blight, and septoria leaf spot, to name a few. If your plant's leaves suddenly have brown curly edges, dark lesions, or "bull's eye" splotches with concentric rings, take a photo of the infected foliage and compare it to images you find online or in a book (your county extension service agent is a good place to start— see our Resources guide for a link). It's normal for leaves to dry out as a plant ages, so do your research to determine whether your plant is indeed infected. Blights are fungal diseases and can spread quickly to fruit and other plants. Sometimes blight can return the following season since the fungi live in the soil. Be prompt and vigilant in treating infected plants. If only a few leaves are affected, there's a good chance you can save the plant. But if most or all of the foliage is diseased, your plant's time is up.

Organic Antidote: Remove affected plant parts and throw them in the trash. You can try applying a commercially available hydrogen peroxide solution to help kill the fungus, if it has only infected small areas of the plant. Overly wet conditions can encourage blight. Preventive techniques include proper watering and spacing plants to allow enough airflow between them. Trim leaves that are touching the ground to prevent soil backsplash from rain and watering. You might also add a layer of mulch around the base of the plant to help your soil retain moisture.

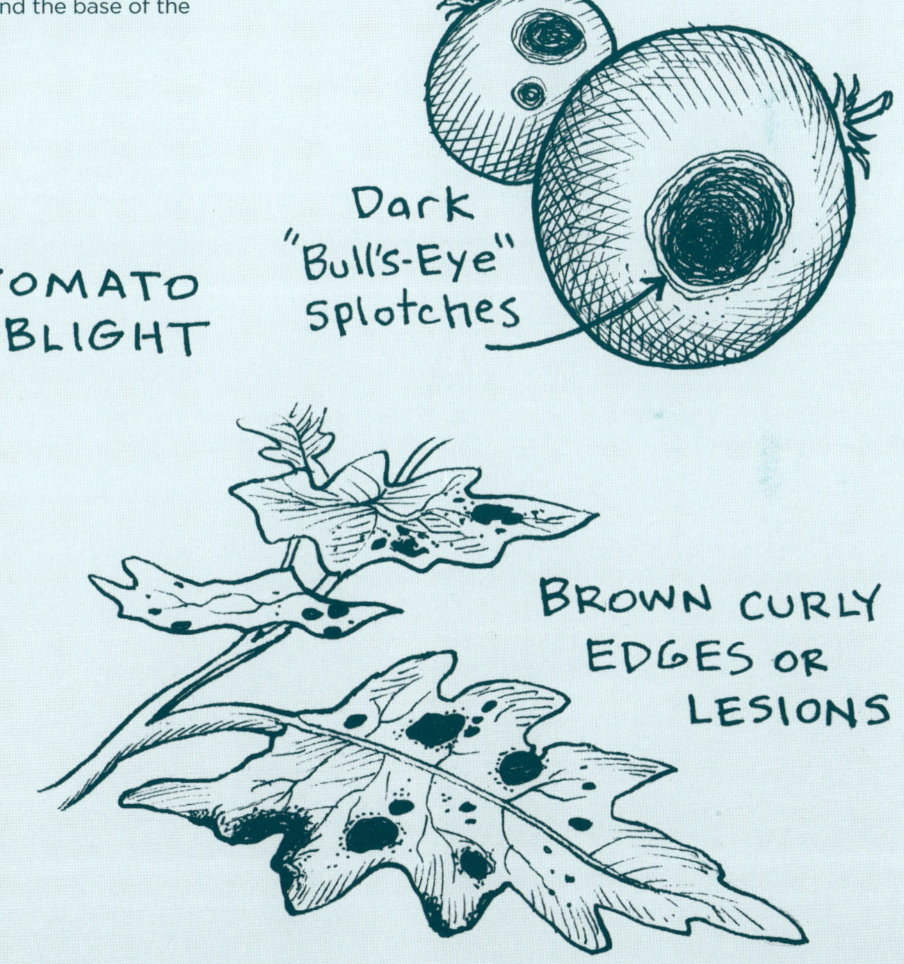

RECIPE BOX

Basil Pesto Sauce

A great alternative to eating basil fresh is to make small batches of pesto sauce. Toss it with your favorite pasta, spread it on sandwiches, layer it into quesadillas ... the uses for pesto are infinite. Our recipe is light on the cheese and nuts — just enough to help form a smooth paste and let the basil shine.

Ingredients

2 cups basil leaves, packed

1–2 garlic cloves

3 tablespoons pine nuts

¼ cup olive oil

2 tablespoons shredded Parmesan or Romano cheese

Salt and freshly ground black pepper

Instructions

Combine basil, garlic, and pine nuts in a food processor or blender. Pulse a few times. Slowly add olive oil while food processor is on. Stop once or twice to scrape down sides of food processor with a rubber spatula. Process until smooth. Add cheese, and salt and pepper to taste. Pulse again until just blended.

Serve immediately or refrigerate in an airtight container with a thin layer of olive oil on top to seal in freshness. Pesto also freezes well; freeze in ice cube trays for smaller portions.

Makes about ½ cup of sauce.

The classic recipe calls for basil and pine nuts. If you want a variation, try substituting other herbs like cilantro or parsley, or other nuts such as walnuts.

Simple Sautéed Greens

Dark leafy greens like kale, collards, and Swiss chard are delicious when cooked. They're great layered into omelettes, tossed into rice and bean bowls, or served as a side dish. Plus, they're packed with nutrition.

Ingredients

6 cups dark leafy greens, spines removed and coarsely chopped

1–2 tablespoons olive oil

Salt and freshly ground black pepper

Instructions

Heat oil in a large skillet over medium heat. Add greens and sauté for 5–7 minutes.* Halfway through cooking, add a dash of salt and pepper. Turn often with tongs or a spatula to ensure even cooking.

Makes 2–3 side servings.

* The greens wilt quickly once you put them in the skillet. You might be surprised to see how much they reduce in size. We like to let them cook awhile until they're well done. Usually the longer you cook greens, the sweeter they taste. Stoves and skillets vary, so if the greens start to get too brown or crispy in those last couple minutes, turn the temperature down to low.

RECIPE BOX

Mixed Green Salad with Strawberries

Nothing says summer like strawberries. Mix them with fresh greens and a tangy dressing for a side dish or light main course. Strawberries sliced crosswise make a lovely presentation and release their juices quickly.

Ingredients

6 cups mixed salad greens

1 sprig fresh mint or tarragon

1 cup strawberries, thinly sliced crosswise

3 tablespoons slivered almonds

2 tablespoons olive oil

2 tablespoons white balsamic vinegar

1 tablespoon Dijon mustard

Salt

Instructions

Remove mint or tarragon leaves from stem and tear into pieces; add to mixed greens. Rinse and drain greens. Set aside.

Toast almonds in a skillet over medium heat for 2–3 minutes, until golden. Stir a couple times to ensure even toasting. Set aside to cool.

In a large bowl, whisk together oil, vinegar, mustard, and a dash of salt. Add greens and almonds and toss until even coated. Serve immediately.

Makes 2 entrée or 4 side servings.

AUGUST 15th
HARVESTED:
17th
GARDEN
JOURNAL

July + August

Ahhh… summer. July and August are the high point of the food gardening season. Amidst your daily tending tasks, you'll have some time to sit back and relax. Take a few moments to acknowledge what you've created. Those tomatoes you've been pampering are plumping up and your cucumbers are multiplying by the minute!

You may feel delighted and a bit overwhelmed by the bounty your small garden has produced. Maybe you simply planted too much (of course you couldn't help yourself — we do it, too!). We'll share some techniques for managing monstrous plants, and we'll offer you lots of recipe ideas.

If you really have gardening fever and want to continue on into fall, now is the time to plan. Reacquaint yourself with those cool crops from the spring and start making your list. Come mid-August, you'll start planting again.

Daily Maintenance

You probably realize by now that food gardening takes some dedication. Watering and other daily maintenance tasks are crucial during the height of the season. This is not to say you shouldn't take a vacation in August. If you aren't home to manage your garden routine, ask someone you trust to water and harvest your ripe veggies. Regular picking will keep your plants productive.

As you proceed through the season, be sure to manage your expectations. Forgive yourself if a vegetable refuses to grow or something fails. Factor in a few losses due to weather, pests, or disease. And try to embrace the "edible aesthetic." In other words, accept that your garden beds may not appear tidy or beautiful all the time, despite your best efforts.

Yes, your garden might look like an overgrown jungle right about now. Around this time of year, plants start to get gangly and foliage dries out. Fruit often doesn't set until late in the plant's life cycle when the rest of the plant looks tangled and unkempt. Use sticks or bamboo stakes to secure peppers and eggplants that are top-heavy. Keep training your winter squash to grow upward (monitor it daily, as tendrils can be hard to unwind once they're set). Make sure any low-lying fruit (like a melon) isn't resting on the ground. Elevating the fruit will help prevent it from rotting or harboring slugs, snails, and pill bugs. If the fruit is heavy, you can place an upside-down pot or layer of straw underneath to keep it from contacting the soil.

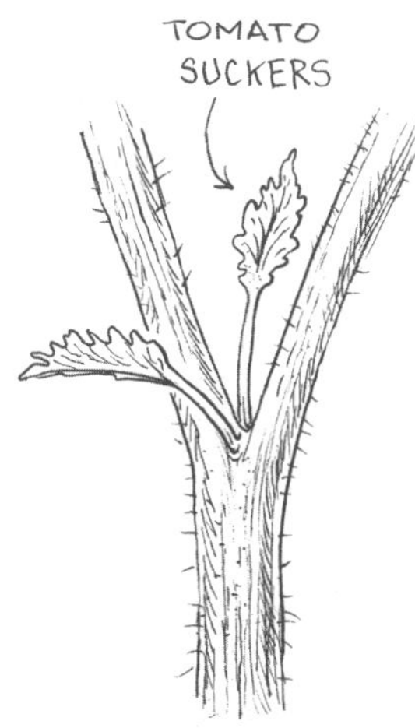

Consider pruning your tomato plants if they're sprawling out of control. But first, a disclaimer: there are many passionate opinions about tomato growing, and techniques for pruning and maintaining tomato plants are as varied as gardeners themselves. You'll develop your own preferences for tomato management as you become more experienced. In keeping with the spirit of this beginner's guide, we advocate one simple pruning technique: removing the "suckers." Suckers are small shoots that form in the joint of a branch and the main stem. Pinch these off or snip them with scissors to keep the plant's energy focused on existing branches and fruit.

Harvest Hints

Come July, your large "slicing" tomatoes — beefsteak, Roma, and the like — are starting to mature. Keep in mind that homegrown tomatoes often don't look like the ones you see in the supermarket. Heirloom varieties, in particular, can take on irregular shapes and sizes. Some varieties are also prone to cracking (but you don't have to throw out a whole tomato just because it's cracked — you can remove the cracked area and eat the rest).

Tomatoes are fully ripe once their color is even, they feel dense and heavy, and yield to gentle pressure. To harvest them, try gently pulling the fruit from the vine by hand. If they don't yield easily, use pruning shears to snip the stems. Pick tomatoes right before you plan to eat them for optimal flavor. If you need to store them, put them on the countertop and not in the fridge, since exposure to cold temperatures can reduce their flavor and texture.

In July and August your beans will ripen so quickly it might be hard to keep up! Pick them often — probably every day — to encourage more production. The smaller the beans, the more tender they'll be. Harvest them before they start to bulge in the pods, and make sure to check under leaves where they can hide from view.

Hot season favorites like eggplants and peppers start to come into their own in mid- to late August. Harvest your eggplants when they're young, shiny, and yield to a gentle squeeze. Peppers can be picked at any time in their growth cycle. In fact, most green peppers are simply red, orange, or yellow (or purple, or chocolate) peppers harvested at a young stage. Pick them at different times for different flavors. In general, the longer you leave bell peppers on the vine, the sweeter they'll be.

For root vegetables, harvesting involves a bit of guesswork. Use a garden spade or fork to gently wedge carrots from the soil, since pulling them by hand can cause the tops to break off and leave the carrots still in the soil. Pull beets and turnips by hand once the roots start to push above the soil and plump up. You can also harvest beet and turnip greens — as long as you don't harm the top of the root, the greens will continue to grow. Wait to harvest onions until the tops die off and the bulbs emerge from the soil, or pull them while they're young and use as scallions.

If you're curious to know how your potatoes are coming along, dig lightly with your hands for a few of the tubers and harvest them as "new" potatoes. They'll be small and tender with thin skins that don't require peeling. After harvesting, push the soil back into place so the remaining potatoes are fully covered. New potatoes don't store well, so they're best enjoyed within a few days. Mature potatoes can be harvested once the plant's foliage has died off (usually sometime in September).

Take care not to harvest your melons too early, since they won't continue to sweeten after they're picked. In late August, you can start inspecting them for signs of readiness. Melons can be a bit tricky. Opinions abound on how to detect their peak ripeness. Usually a watermelon is ripe when its tendril at the stem turns from bright green to brown, when the skin is hard enough to resist an indentation from your fingernail, and when the melon's surface changes from shiny to dull. When inspecting cantaloupes, look for rinds that have changed from green to tan or yellow, and cracks in the stems that attach to the fruit. Give the cantaloupe a soft tap and it should sound hollow, and if it's making you crazy with its heavenly perfume, it's probably ready. Harvest melons by cutting the fruit at the stem with pruning shears.

In general, it's best to pick your fruits and veggies early in the morning when temperatures are cool. At this time of day, they'll be at their peak flavor and freshness. By midday, plants are stressed from the heat and are more likely to wilt or go limp after they're picked. This is especially true for leafy

FALL CROPS

Come mid-August, you'll decide whether to plant another round of crops for fall. You may feel tired at this point in the season, so if you opt out, you're no less of a gardener. If you want to keep the momentum going, revisit your list of cool season crops and their maturity times (look back to March to find these). Then work backwards from the first frost date (October 23rd, on average) to determine when you should plant. Note that while spring and fall temperatures are similar, fall days are shorter, which means less sun exposure. For crops that take longer than 60 days to mature, you're best starting from seedlings.

greens and herbs. If you're not an early bird or gardening in the morning doesn't fit into your schedule, do your picking at dusk or right before dinnertime.

At the height of the season, you may find yourself harvesting more than you can comfortably eat. Give your surplus produce to friends or neighbors — and show off your gardening skills in the process! Or consider donating it to a local food pantry, where fresh produce is often in short supply (see our Resources section for more information). You can also try your hand at preserving your harvest for fall and winter (look ahead to September for tips).

Edible Flowers

You might be surprised to know that some flowers are actually edible! Flowers add color and elegance to any dish. Sprinkle them on salads, pair them with cheese, or use them to garnish cakes and other desserts — be creative.

Most flowers don't last long after they're picked, so harvest them right before you plan to eat them, if possible. If you need to store them for a few hours, cut them with the stems intact and place in a glass of water, or between damp paper towels in the fridge. Make sure to wash and inspect flowers thoroughly prior to eating, since bugs often like to hide inside.

If you're allergy-prone, you might want to steer clear of eating flowers, or at least start with a very small amount, since they contain pollen. And of course, only eat a flower if you're sure it's safe to eat.

These are some popular edible flowers and their flavors:

Flower	Flavor
Borage	Cucumber
Chives	Garlic, onion
Cornflowers (Bachelor's Buttons)	Spicy, clove
Lavender	Aromatic
Nasturtiums	Peppery, radish
Pansies	Mild, green
Squash blossoms (blossoms only; remove stamens)	Sweet, squash
Sunflower buds (before flowers open)	Artichoke
Sunflower petals	Bittersweet
Violets	Sweet

RECIPE BOX

Tomato Bruschetta

Bruschetta is a summer staple we never get tired of (in fact, we find it highly addictive). It's easy to prepare again and again throughout the season as your tomato harvest keeps on going. Tomatoes and basil are the stars here, with only light seasoning required.

Ingredients

4 medium Roma, heirloom, or other "slicing" tomatoes, finely chopped

8–10 large basil leaves, torn into pieces or cut in a chiffonade*

2 garlic cloves, minced

1 teaspoon olive oil

1 teaspoon balsamic vinegar

Salt and freshly ground black pepper

Baguette or crusty bread

Instructions

Combine tomatoes, basil, garlic, olive oil, and vinegar. Add salt and pepper to taste. Let stand at room temperature for at least 20 minutes for flavors to combine. Meanwhile, cut bread into slices and toast. Spoon tomato mixture on top of bread slices. Best enjoyed immediately.

Serves 4.

* "Chiffonade" is a cutting technique (the word "chiffon" is French for "little rag"—it describes the long rag-like strips that result from this technique). It sounds fancy, but it's actually really simple. Just stack the basil leaves, roll them into a bundle, and then cut the bundle into thin slices. You can use this method for other leafy herbs and greens as well.

Garlic Green Beans

Love garlic? We do, too. Pair it generously with your green beans for a heavenly side dish.

Ingredients

4 cups green beans, ends removed

8–10 garlic cloves, halved or quartered

1–2 tablespoons olive oil

Salt and freshly ground black pepper

Instructions

Heat oil in a large skillet over medium heat. Add green beans and cover with a lid or splatter screen; cook for about 2 minutes. Remove cover and add a dash of salt and pepper; cook for 5–6 more minutes. Add garlic and cook for 1–2 more minutes, until garlic is golden and beans are tender, lightly browned, and starting to wrinkle. Stir frequently to ensure even cooking.

Serves 4.

CHIFFONADE

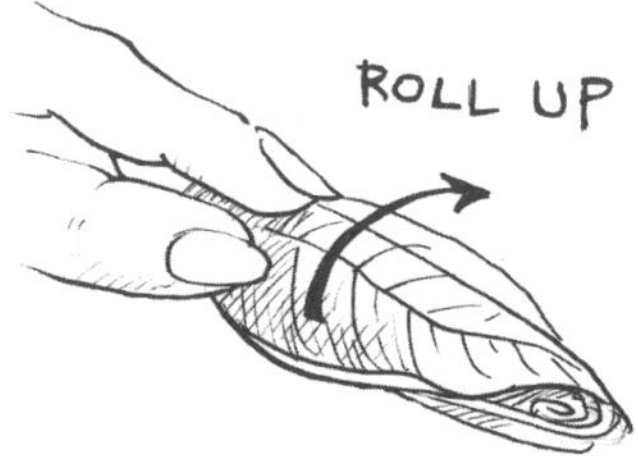

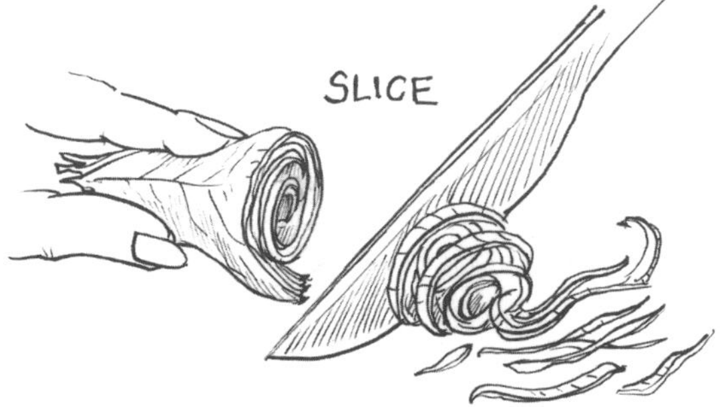

RECIPE BOX

Cucumber Mint Salad

Enjoy this cool salad on a really hot day. It's perfect for picnics and backyard barbecues. Serve with pita bread or as a fresh companion to grilled meats. Add chickpeas or couscous for a heartier salad.

Ingredients

2 medium cucumbers, peeled, seeded, and cut into ½-inch chunks

1 ½ cups cherry tomatoes, halved*

¼ cup mint leaves, torn into small pieces

½ cup crumbed feta cheese

2 tablespoons olive oil

2 tablespoons white wine vinegar

Salt and freshly ground black pepper

Instructions

In a large bowl, whisk together oil and vinegar, and salt and pepper to taste. Add cucumbers, tomatoes, mint, and cheese. Stir until just blended. Serve immediately.

Serves 4.

* For a variety of colors and shapes, use a mix of small tomatoes (yellow pear, red grape, etc.).

Zucchini Bread!

Zucchini Bread

What to do with all this zucchini? Make zucchini bread, of course! This recipe makes two loaves. Enjoy one now and freeze the other for later. Home-baked goodies also make great gifts.

Ingredients

2 teaspoons butter, softened

2 tablespoons + 2 cups unbleached all-purpose flour

1 cup whole wheat flour

1 teaspoon baking powder

1 teaspoon baking soda

1 teaspoon salt

1 tablespoon cinnamon

2 cups shredded zucchini

2 eggs, beaten

1 cup sugar

½ cup honey

1 cup canola or safflower oil

1 tablespoon vanilla extract

1 cup walnuts, finely chopped

1 cup raisins (or substitute chocolate chips)

Instructions

Preheat oven to 350.° Grease and flour two 8½ x 4½ loaf pans.* Place a teaspoon of softened butter in each pan; spread butter to coat interior of pans, using a small plastic bag or piece of wax paper to keep your fingers clean. Sprinkle a tablespoon of flour in each pan, then tilt and tap pans so flour distributes over entire greased area. Dump excess flour in the sink or trash.

In a large bowl, combine flour, baking powder, baking soda, salt, and cinnamon; stir well. In a separate bowl, combine zucchini, eggs, sugar, honey, oil, and vanilla. Pour liquids over flour mixture and stir until just moistened. Gently fold in walnuts and raisins. Do not overmix.

Spoon batter into pans. Bake for 1 hour or until a toothpick inserted in center of each loaf comes out clean (a small crack down the center of the loaf is normal). Allow loaves to cool in pans. Remove from pans and slice when completely cool. For 9" x 5" pans, reduce baking time by 10 minutes.

Makes 2 loaves, with about 8 slices per loaf.

* Greasing and flouring the pans will ensure that the breads release easily from the pans once they're cool.

September

With Labor Day comes the unofficial beginning of fall. Vacations have come and gone, kids go back to school, and work routines resume. September can be a melancholy time as the daylight starts to dwindle. But rest assured your garden will still be pumping out the good stuff during these last few hot weeks.

This month we'll give you tips on late season harvesting and garden maintenance. And we'll give you more ideas on what to do with all this awesome food. Don't worry — you don't have to eat it all now. There are a number of ways you can preserve your harvest and make it last for months to come!

Harvest and Maintenance

In this final stretch of the growing season, your plants will put one last push into fruiting. For crops that are still maturing — like peppers, eggplants, melons, winter squash, and indeterminate tomatoes — pinch off any new blossoms that you see to direct the plant's energy toward ripening existing fruit, rather than producing new fruit. There isn't enough time left in the season for new fruit to fully ripen.

Observing the life cycle of winter squash can be a good test of your patience. Don't be tempted to pick them early. They're worth the wait! When the vine starts to die, they'll be ready to harvest. This usually happens in late October or near the first frost. We'll get to harvesting details next month, so just keep watch on them for now.

Potatoes should be fully mature this month once their foliage dies off. To harvest them, dig carefully in the soil around the plants, either by hand or with a garden spade or fork. Start from the outside to avoid cutting or bruising the tubers. You can also gently pull up the entire plant, and most of the potatoes will remain attached. Make sure to dig around in the soil one more time to find any stragglers.

It's okay if you end up with some bruised or cut spuds. Just make sure to eat them right away, since they won't keep for very long. Otherwise you can store potatoes that are in good condition. First let them sit or "cure" for a week or two at room temperature. Then place them in a burlap or brown paper bag with holes to protect them from light, which can cause them to turn green and taste bitter. Green potatoes also contain a toxic chemical that can cause indigestion, so it's best to avoid eating them. Transfer your tubers to a cool, humid location (40 – 45° is ideal), and they'll keep for up to two months.

Other root vegetables such as carrots, beets, turnips, and onions can be harvested as needed. Or you can leave them in the ground for a few more weeks, since they can tolerate cooler temperatures. Like potatoes, if you plan to store onions, make sure to cure them first. Exposure to warm temperatures for 1 – 2 weeks will thicken their skins and heal surface wounds. Don't wash root vegetables (potatoes included) until you're ready to use them, since the added moisture can encourage mold growth. Also, avoid storing potatoes and onions together, as each one emits a gas that causes the other to spoil faster than normal.

You're probably still getting some beans at this point. As an alterative to picking them fresh, you can wait until the beans bulge and mature inside the pods. The pods will be green and inedible, but you can still shell the beans and cook them (they're actually called "shelly" beans at this stage). Or you can let the pods stay on the vine until they turn brown and dry out completely, and either harvest and prepare them as you would other dry beans, or save them for next year's sowing.

If you have plants that are no longer bearing fruit, you can go ahead and remove them. Even if their foliage looks green and healthy, it's too late in the season for these plants to produce fruit of edible size. Avoid pulling up plants by hand unless they're root vegetables or have small root systems. Uprooting a plant in this way — especially a large, heavily rooted one — can disrupt your soil balance, and make a big mess in the process. It's best to remove plants by cutting their stems at the soil level with pruning shears (for stems that are tough, use loppers or a hand saw). The remaining roots should break down into the soil by the time you're ready to plant again in the spring (see the "Garden Clean-Up" section on page 63 for more tips).

Preserving Your Harvest

If you can't possibly consume all your fruits and veggies while they're still fresh — don't worry! There are a variety of ways to preserve your harvest and extend its life for weeks or even months to come. Some preservation techniques actually transform your food, imparting new flavors and textures distinct from their fresh counterparts.

Freezing is probably the easiest method of preservation. Just make sure to plan ahead and leave plenty of space in your freezer. Most of the time, freezing doesn't require much prepwork — just some slicing or chopping, then transferring vegetable pieces into a freezer bag or other freezer-safe container. Zucchini is great shredded and frozen for use in baked goods and lasagna. Chopped kale defrosts quickly and makes a healthy addition to soups and stir-fries. For hot peppers, a little goes a long way. Finely chop or purée the peppers, spoon into ice cube trays to freeze, then pop out the cubes once they're solid and store in a freezer bag. Or sandwich spoonfuls of the purée between squares of plastic wrap or aluminum foil, and defrost individually as needed.

BLANCHING TOMATOES

Frozen tomatoes are great to have on hand for winter soups and stews. Paste and beefsteak varieties take well to freezing, while cherry tomatoes don't (enjoy these while they're still fresh). Tomato skins don't break down well when cooked, so we suggest "blanching" your tomatoes to remove their skins from the flesh, prior to freezing.

The blanching process is quick and easy. Prepare your tomatoes by cutting out the stems. Using a slotted spoon, lower the fruit into a pan of boiling water, with only a few tomatoes in the pan at a time. Leave them for about a minute (you might see the skins start to crack or peel back from the top), then transfer them into a bowl of ice water to stop them from cooking. Once the tomatoes are cool, peel off the skins by hand. You can freeze them whole or cut them in half, remove the seeds, and freeze the halves.

Since tomatoes are juicy, they have a tendency to stick together as they freeze. To keep the pieces from turning into one big chunk, arrange them in a single layer on a baking pan to freeze. Once they're frozen solid, transfer them into a freezer bag, and you can pull them out one at a time as needed.

If you don't want to spend time blanching your tomatoes, it's okay to freeze them whole with the skins on. When you're ready to use them, let them thaw out first and then peel off the skins with a knife. This method requires a bit more peeling than a blanched tomato, but works just fine.

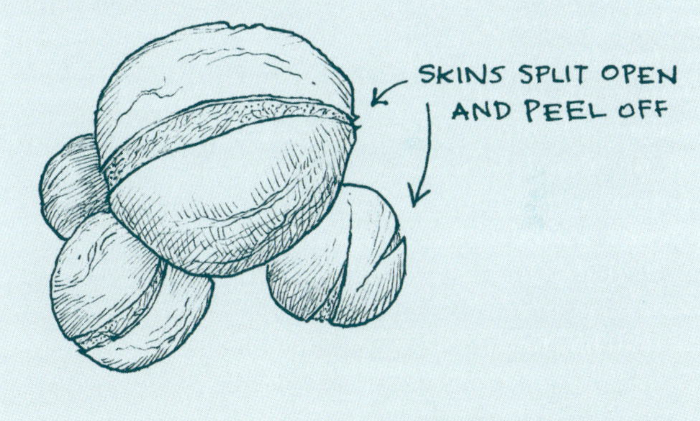

Drying is an age-old form of food preservation. Reducing the moisture content in foods helps prevent the growth of bacteria, mold, and yeast that would otherwise cause spoilage. You can dry your harvest in several different ways.

Herbs are well suited for air drying. Harvest them with as much stem attached as you can. If they're dirty, rinse them in cool water and shake them gently to remove excess moisture. Then tie the stems together in small bundles and hang them upside down to dry. Choose an indoor spot that's well ventilated and warm (avoid direct sunlight, which can sap herbs of their color and flavor). Once the herbs are fully dried, store them whole in airtight containers in a cool, dark place. Crush or crumble them just prior to using for freshest flavor.

Fruits and veggies can be oven-dried and either eaten as snacks or re-hydrated for later use. Small vegetables like peas and beans can be dried whole, while others such as tomatoes and carrots need to be sliced first. Some vegetables should be blanched prior to drying to help preserve their color and flavor. Small chili peppers dry beautifully and can be crushed or ground for use in seasoning.

Successful oven-drying requires a very low temperature — usually somewhere between 125° and 200° — to avoid cooking the food (some ovens have a "dehydrate" function, which allows for small temperature adjustments within this range). Drying times can last from 3 to 12 or more hours, depending on the moisture content and size of the food. Check your oven manual or look online to find drying times and temperatures for specific fruits and veggies. Once you've prepped your food for drying, spread it in a single layer on a baking sheet and place it in a preheated oven. Prop open the oven door with a wooden spoon to help increase air circulation and hasten drying. Check the food periodically and turn it every few hours to ensure even drying. When the pieces feel leathery, without any moisture, chances are they're done.

If your oven isn't equipped for dehydration, or if you don't want to leave your oven on for long stretches of time with the door ajar, you can try using an electric food dehydrator. This small countertop appliance usually consists of several drying trays, a heat source, and a fan for circulating air. A food dehydrator isn't a "must-have" device. But it can save you time and free up your oven for other baking needs. And it's a safe alterative to oven-drying if you have young children running around the kitchen.

Pickling and canning are other time-honored ways of preserving food. These techniques have enjoyed a resurgence in recent years, along with a rise in curiosity and appreciation for old-fashioned tastes.

The pickling process is fairly simple. While individual recipes vary, the basic technique (often referred to as "hot packing") involves boiling a mixture of water, vinegar, and salt, which is poured over vegetables packed into glass canning jars. Once the jars are sealed, they can be stored

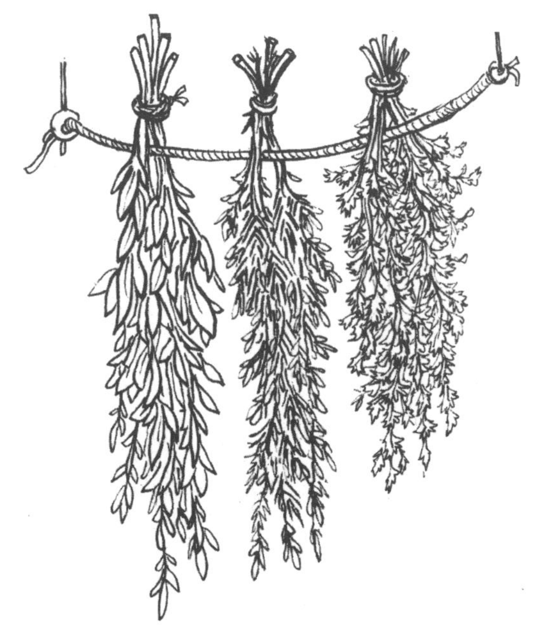

in the refrigerator for several weeks. The acidic brine acts as a natural preservative. Cucumbers are an obvious favorite for pickling, but many other vegetables are tasty when pickled — beans, onions, and cauliflower, to name a few. You can also experiment with different veggie combinations and use herbs or spices to enhance flavor.

Canning is the most labor-intensive method of food preservation. It requires some special equipment and a commitment to learning proper techniques. For many home gardeners, it's worth the investment of time and resources. Canned foods can store for up to a year and make memorable gifts for any occasion.

The basic canning process (called "water bath" canning) involves cooking your food, sealing it in glass canning jars or other sterile containers, and boiling the containers to kill and inhibit the growth of bacteria and other microorganisms. Each fruit or veggie requires a specific boiling time based on its natural acidic content. In general, high-acid foods don't spoil as easily and are boiled for less time. Low-acid foods need the addition of lemon juice, citric acid, or vinegar to increase acidity levels, or may require additional treatment in a device called a pressure canner.

Canned foods carry a higher risk of contamination and spoilage than other preserved foods. Your work area should be very clean, and special care must be taken to properly handle your food, sterilize equipment, and process foods according to required times and temperatures. To learn how to can, we recommend taking a hands-on course taught by an expert or purchasing a book on canning from a reputable source (make sure it was published in 1989 or later to comply with current USDA guidelines).

Hopefully this overview has sparked your interest in food preservation! See the Resources section if you want to learn more.

RECIPE BOX

Pico de Gallo

This fresh salsa packs a punch and it's simple to prepare. Use it to dress your tacos or burgers, and of course, heap it onto your favorite chips.

Ingredients

4 medium ripe tomatoes, seeded and finely chopped

1 small white onion, finely chopped

¾ cup cilantro leaves, coarsely chopped

2 jalapeño peppers, finely chopped (for less heat, remove seeds before chopping)

2 tablespoons fresh lime juice

Salt to taste

Instructions

Combine ingredients. Cover and refrigerate for at least 30 minutes to let flavors combine. Best enjoyed right away.

Makes about 2½ cups of salsa.

Marinara Sauce

If you have tomatoes coming out your ears, make some sauce! Here's a basic marinara with a bit of spice. It's typically served over pasta, but you might also try it with spaghetti squash or as a dip for appetizers. It freezes well — and will come in handy when you need to fix dinner in a jiffy.

Ingredients

¼ cup olive oil

8 cloves garlic, minced

10 – 12 Roma or other slicing tomatoes (about 3 pounds), peeled* and seeded

Dried red pepper flakes (optional)

Salt

10 large basil leaves, torn into small pieces

Instructions

Heat oil in a large saucepan over medium heat. Add garlic and cook until lightly browned, about 2 minutes. Add tomatoes and bring to a boil. Season with salt and red pepper to taste. Lower heat to a simmer. Use a spoon or potato masher to break up tomatoes into chunks. Cook until sauce is thick, about 20 minutes. Stir in basil 5 minutes before sauce is done cooking.

Makes about 4 cups of sauce, or enough for 6 – 8 servings.

* Peel the tomatoes with a paring knife, or blanch them to remove the peelings (look back to the "Blanching Tomatoes" section to learn how).

RECIPE BOX

Baked Eggplant Cutlets

This is an old family recipe once referred to as "Eggplant Hater's Eggplant." Even eggplant skeptics will find this preparation rich and tasty.

Ingredients

1 medium eggplant, peeled and cut into ¼-inch slices

⅔ cup mayonnaise

1½ cups cornflakes

1 cup prepared bread crumbs, or 1–2 pieces of bread

½ cup grated Parmesan cheese

Salt and fresh ground pepper

Instructions

Preheat oven to 425°. With a blender or food processor, process cornflakes into coarse crumbs; add prepared bread crumbs and process until mixed. Alternately, tear 1–2 pieces of bread into small pieces and process into coarse crumbs; add cornflakes and process until texture is even. Add cheese, and salt and pepper to taste; process until combined.

Pour mayonnaise into a shallow bowl; pour breading mixture into a shallow bowl or onto a plate. Working one slice at a time, coat eggplant with mayonnaise, cover with breading, then arrange onto a baking sheet. Bake for 20 minutes, or until eggplant is tender and browned on top.

Best enjoyed immediately. Reheat leftovers in oven or toaster oven to revive crispiness.

Serves 4–6.

Cornbread Muffins with Poblano Peppers

Cornbread ranks high on our list of comfort foods. We like to mix in some sweet corn and peppers for added flavor and texture. Poblanos give a touch of heat. If you want to turn it up a notch, substitute serranos or jalapeños.

Ingredients

1 cup all-purpose flour

1 cup medium grind yellow cornmeal

3 teaspoons baking powder

½ teaspoon salt

5 tablespoons butter, softened

2 tablespoons sugar

1 egg, beaten

1 cup milk

½ poblano pepper, finely chopped (about ½ cup)

1 ear fresh sweet corn

Instructions

Preheat oven to 400°. While oven is preheating, cook unhusked corn in microwave for 3–4 minutes. Wearing oven mitts to protect your hands, remove corn from microwave and place on cutting board. Cut the bottom inch off, then shake to release cob from husk. Run cob under cold water or set aside to cool.

In a large bowl, combine flour, cornmeal, baking powder, and salt; stir well. In a separate bowl, combine butter and sugar; add egg and milk, and stir well. Pour liquid mixture over flour mixture and stir until lumpy.

Position corn on cutting board, cut side down. Start at the top and saw downward to remove kernels from ear. Fold corn and peppers into muffin batter until just combined. Do not overmix.

Spoon batter into 12-cup non-stick muffin pan. Bake for 20–25 minutes, until golden and cracked on top.

Makes 12 muffins.

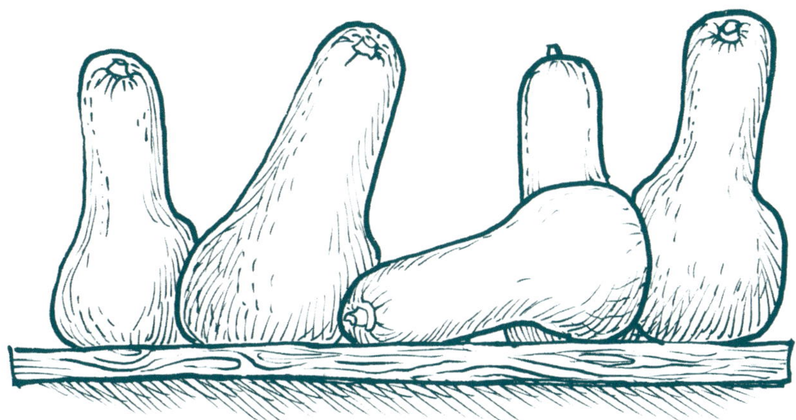

October

October usually marks the close of Chicago's growing season. You might feel relieved or even a little sad that things are finally winding down, after months of lovingly tending your garden. Our first frost usually arrives around October 23rd.

This month you'll need to start monitoring the weather closely from day to day. Be ready to harvest most of your remaining veggies on short notice. Some of your plants won't mind a light frost. But for many of them, it means game over. We'll help you distinguish which ones to harvest and which ones you can leave on the vine a little while longer.

Toward the end of October (and into November), you'll have some cleaning up to do. We'll give you tips on how to clear out your raised beds and prepare them for winter. And we'll advise on how to compost your garden trimmings, so little is left to waste.

First Frost

In food gardening terms, there are two levels of frost: "light" frost, which forms between temperatures of 28° and 32°; and "hard" frost (sometimes called "killing" frost), which occurs below 28°. Tender crops like tomatoes and basil usually are damaged by light frost. Semi-hardy and hardy crops like kale and cabbage often can withstand light or even hard frost. Below 25° is dangerous territory for most edible plants.

Frost doesn't necessarily occur just because the air temperature drops to 32°. Whether frost forms depends on a combination of factors, including soil temperature, humidity, and air movement. In early fall, the soil still retains warmth and can radiate heat, so plants and fruit that are close to the ground are less likely to be affected by frost. Humid air also can help insulate against frost, as it holds more heat that dry air. If your garden beds are situated next to your house or another structure, they have added protection against frost. These structures can retain heat during the day and radiate it outward, and they also act as windbreaks. In more open areas, wind can sweep away warm air near the ground and increase the likelihood of frost.

Keep an eye on your nighttime forecast, since frost is most likely to form overnight when the temperature dips down. If there's any chance of frost on a given night, harvest your most tender crops that day. You can use a floating row cover to help protect your plants from a light frost. While row covers don't completely insure against frost damage, they do give your plants a fighting chance and can help extend your growing season a bit.

FROST TOLERANCE OF VEGETABLES

Sensitive (damaged by light frost)	Semi-hardy (can tolerate light frost)	Hardy (can tolerate hard frost)
• Basil	• Arugula	• Broccoli
• Beans	• Beets	• Brussels sprouts
• Cucumbers	• Carrots	• Cabbage
• Eggplants	• Cauliflower	• Collards
• Okra	• Celery	• Kale
• Peppers	• Lettuce	• Kohlrabi
• Summer squash	• Peas	• Onions
• Tomatillos	• Swiss chard	• Parsley
• Tomatoes		• Radishes
• Melons		• Spinach
		• Turnips
		• Leeks

LEVELS OF FROST

Light frost = 28° to 32°

Hard frost = Below 28°

Last Harvest

Fruit-bearing hot crops like tomatoes and peppers are highly sensitive to frost. Exposure to cold temperatures will cause them to become mushy and diminish their flavor, so harvest these prior to any chance of frost.

On the other hand, don't be in a hurry to harvest your cool crops. Brussels sprouts, kale, and other hardy greens are cold-resistant and actually grow sweeter when exposed to cold temperatures. The same is true for most root vegetables. Their tops may die off, but the roots will be safe nestled in the soil. It's worth it to leave some of your cool crops in the ground for a few more weeks, or at least through periods of light to moderate frost.

While peas can withstand periods of light frost, they usually don't mature as quickly in the fall as they did in the spring. Even if you don't see any pea pods forming on the plants, you can still eat the leaves, stems, and tendrils. Snip off the top few inches of growth, or "shoots," from the vines while they're young and tender, and prepare them as you would other greens (they'll taste like peas!).

You can extend the life of most herbs by bringing them indoors for the winter. If your herbs are already in containers, dig out the plants and re-pot them in fresh soil before taking them inside (your outdoor soil might contain insects). Transfer herbs from your raised beds into pots using new soil as well. If situated near a south-facing window, herbs can live for many weeks, and can sometimes "overwinter" and return to their outdoor habitat in the spring.

Alternatively, you can let annual herbs such as dill and cilantro remain outside and "go to seed." They'll end up dropping seeds and "self-sowing," which means you won't have to plant them again next season. You can also leave perennial herbs like mint, chives, and sage outside in their containers or beds. They'll die off and then return again in the spring.

Finally, the time has come to harvest your winter squash! Harvest them before the first frost, once the vine starts to dry out and turn brown. Use pruning shears to cut the squash from the vine, leaving a couple inches of the stems attached to help prevent bacterial infection. Cure your squash for 1 – 2 weeks at 70 – 80° to help thicken their skins so they'll store longer. It's okay to leave them outside in the daytime sun, but take them indoors at night when temperatures dip down and critters get curious. If properly cured and stored, butternut squash will last for up to three months, and other varieties such as Hubbard can last up to six months.

Yes, you can still eat from your garden in January! Squash, as well as potatoes, onions, carrots, and other root crops, can be enjoyed throughout the winter if they're stored well. The best location for "cold" storage is a dark, unheated spot such as your basement, mud room, or crawl space.

Carefully inspect your vegetables prior to storage, and only store those in good condition. Any soft spots, cuts, or bruises can lead to infection, and infection can spread to other vegetables (it's true — one "bad apple" can spoil the whole bunch). Don't wash anything that you plan to store, as the added moisture can encourage the growth of mold. Make sure to cure onions and potatoes before storing them away, and locate them separately from each other for prolonged life. Prepare carrots, beets, and turnips by trimming off their tops, leaving a small stub intact.

GREEN TOMATOES

What to do with all those green tomatoes still waiting on the vine? No need to toss them. You have a couple choices.

Your first option is to pick the tomatoes and eat them. Green tomatoes aren't sweet and juicy like their vine-ripened counterparts. Their texture is firm and their flavor is sour—not the best for eating raw. But they do lend well to cooking (you've probably heard of "fried green tomatoes"). Green tomatoes are delicious in their own right, and they're a nice treat to mark the end of the growing season and arrival of fall.

If eating green tomatoes doesn't sound appealing, you can still harvest them and take them indoors to ripen. Tomatoes even with a tinge of color will probably ripen, if given time. The simplest method is to set them on your countertop away from direct sunlight—and wait. Be patient, as they might take a couple weeks to change color.

You can try to speed up the process by placing the tomatoes in a brown paper bag with a banana, which gives off ethylene gas and can hasten ripening (if the banana rots before the tomatoes ripen, replace the banana). Or you can wrap the tomatoes in newspaper and place them in a box. Store the covered tomatoes in a warm area away from direct sunlight, and check them every day or two to see how they're coming along.

Don't be disappointed if not all of your green tomatoes ripen, and don't expect them to taste like the vine-ripened ones you picked last month. But they still might be better than what you'd buy in the supermarket, or at least good enough to freeze for use in soups and stews.

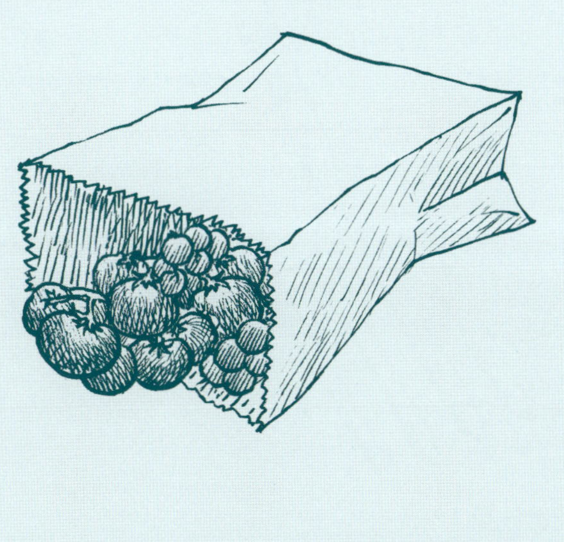

Veggies can be stored in a variety of containers. Pile them into baskets, wooden crates, metal bins, or cardboard boxes with holes cut in them for ventilation. Keep your containers on a shelf, or at least off the floor, to discourage furry foragers from enjoying your hard work. Onions, in particular, can be hung in mesh bags or old pantyhose. Leeks and root crops like carrots and parsnips can be insulated with sawdust (or straw) to help preserve moisture content. Just add a couple inches of the sawdust to the bottom and sides of your container (you can line it first with burlap or newspaper to keep the sawdust from spilling out the sides). Pack in a layer of veggies, cover with a bit of sawdust, and continue alternating layers.

Of course, don't feel obligated to store your veggies. If you only harvested a few carrots, enjoy them right away. But if you ended up with 10 pounds, then winter storage might be a good option.

Garden Clean-Up

You've worked hard all season. Give yourself a break, if you haven't already! Chicago weather can stay mild into November, so there's no need to rush clearing out your garden beds. You might tidy up in stages as your plants start to die off, or save it all for a sunny day when you have the time.

When removing spent plants, avoid pulling them out by hand. Uprooting plants, especially ones with large root systems like tomatoes and squash, can be difficult and messy. But more importantly, turning the soil in this way is disruptive to your soil balance. All those tiny soil-dwelling organisms are doing a fine job conditioning your soil and keeping it healthy, so disturb them as little as possible. Use pruning shears to cut off your plants at the soil level, and the roots that remain should break down into the soil by next spring.

“But it’s the end of the season. Why should I care about my soil now?” you might ask. Because with a raised bed, you use the same soil from year to year. Taking special measures to nurture your soil — before, during, and after the growing season — can dramatically improve the health of your garden for years to come.

Most of your garden “waste” can actually be recycled. We recommend composting it rather than throwing it the trash. Simply cut your trimmings into small pieces and spread them directly back over your soil. They’ll start to decompose and immediately return nutrients to the soil (this is a form of “passive” composting, as it requires little effort on your part, except to set the process in motion and let nature do the work). The trimmings will also act as mulch to help insulate your beds over the winter. If any pieces remain in the spring, you can remove them or gently mix them into the top layer of your soil.

Some gardeners choose to compost continually throughout the year (not only at the end of the growing season) and find it a very meaningful practice. Fall is an opportune time to start, since you’ll likely have a surplus of garden waste you can use as raw materials. If year-round composting sounds appealing to you, see the Beyond the Basics chapter for more details.

You can compost all plant parts — leaves, stems, roots, unripe and overripe fruit — as long as they haven’t been affected by disease or pests. Sometimes bacteria and fungi can survive the winter, and bug larvae can linger on plants and emerge again in the spring. You don’t want any of that stuff coming back into your garden, so make sure to discard affected plant parts in the trash. Some organisms can also overwinter in the soil, especially if temperatures are mild. If you have diseased or pest-ridden areas of soil, remove them and put them in the trash, too. And set aside any stakes, trellises, or tools that came in contact with diseased plants, as you’ll need to disinfect them (look to November/December for tips).

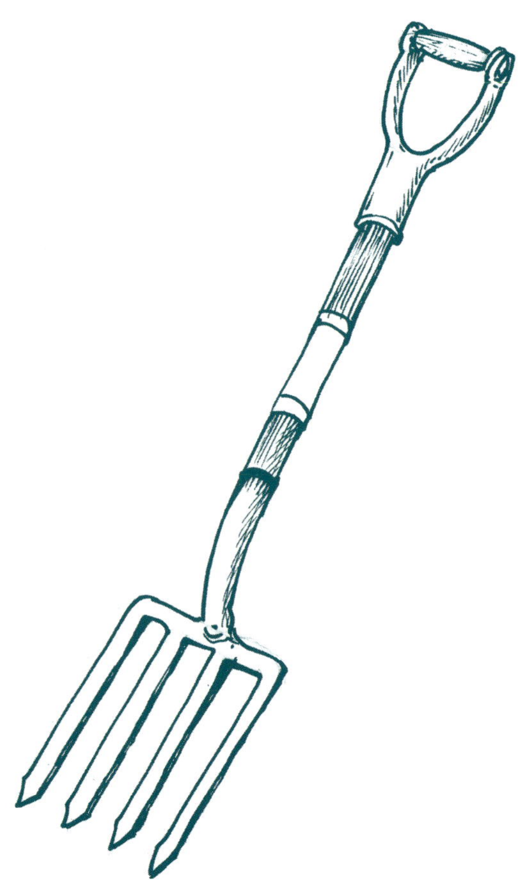

RECIPE BOX

White Bean and Sage Salad

Smooth beans and subtle herb flavor make this salad a versatile companion to any main course. It's quick and easy to prepare. For a variation, try substituting thyme or tarragon.

Ingredients

2 15-ounce cans navy or cannellini beans, drained

10 – 12 fresh sage leaves, cut in chiffonade*

1 cup cherry tomatoes, halved

½ cup celery, finely chopped

3 tablespoons olive oil

3 tablespoons white wine vinegar

Salt and freshly ground black pepper

Instructions

Combine beans, sage, tomatoes, celery, oil, and vinegar. Add salt and pepper to taste. Let sit at room temperature for 20 minutes so flavors combine.

Serves 4 – 6.

* See "Tomato Bruschetta" recipe in July/August for instructions.

Herb Roasted Potatoes

There are countless ways to enjoy potatoes. Roasting is one of our favorite preparations — it really brings out the spuds' natural sweetness. In this recipe, we add garlic and parsley. If you like your potatoes plain and simple, then pass on these additions.

Ingredients

4 medium potatoes

3 garlic cloves, minced

1 cup parsley, coarsely chopped

2 tablespoons olive oil

Salt and freshly ground black pepper

Instructions

Preheat oven to 425°. While oven is preheating, scrub potatoes and cut into 1½-inch chunks. In a large bowl, combine potatoes, olive oil, and a dash of salt and pepper; toss to coat. Spread in a single layer onto a large baking sheet. Prepare garlic and parsley; mix together in a small bowl and set aside.

Bake potatoes for 40 – 45 minutes; stir once with a spatula halfway through, then twice during second half of cooking, to ensure even browning. Bake until crispy and browned.

Remove potatoes from oven. Pour herb mixture over potatoes, and stir to coat. Return to oven and bake for 3 – 5 more minutes, or until greens are wilted and garlic is translucent.

Best enjoyed immediately. Reheat leftovers in oven or toaster oven to revive crispiness.

Serves 4.

RECIPE BOX

Root Vegetable Salad

Root veggies are often under-appreciated in garden fare. But these sweet and earthy bulbs are worth your attention. You might be surprised by how tasty they are, especially when eaten raw. In this salad, we add kale and broccoli stalks to the mix (yes, you can eat broccoli stalks!).

Ingredients

2–3 large kale leaves

1 medium golden beet

1 medium turnip

2 large broccoli stalks

3 small kohlrabi bulbs

2 large carrots

¼ cup pistachios, coarsely chopped

3 tablespoons olive oil

3 tablespoons white wine vinegar

Salt and freshly ground black pepper

Instructions

Toast pistachios in a skillet over medium heat for 2–3 minutes, until golden. Stir a couple times to ensure even toasting. Set aside to cool.

Remove spines from kale and finely shred. With a paring knife, remove peelings from beet, turnip, broccoli stalks, and kohlrabi.* Peel carrots with a vegetable peeler. Using a mandolin or vegetable peeler, shave remaining vegetables into very thin slices.

In a large bowl, whisk together oil and vinegar, and salt and pepper to taste. Add vegetables and pistachios; toss to coat. Let sit at room temperature for 20–30 minutes so vegetables soften slightly and flavors combine.

Best enjoyed immediately, but also will keep for a day in the fridge.

Serves 4.

* Kohlrabi and broccoli stalks sometimes have a tough, woody layer just underneath their skins. Make sure to peel off this layer as well.

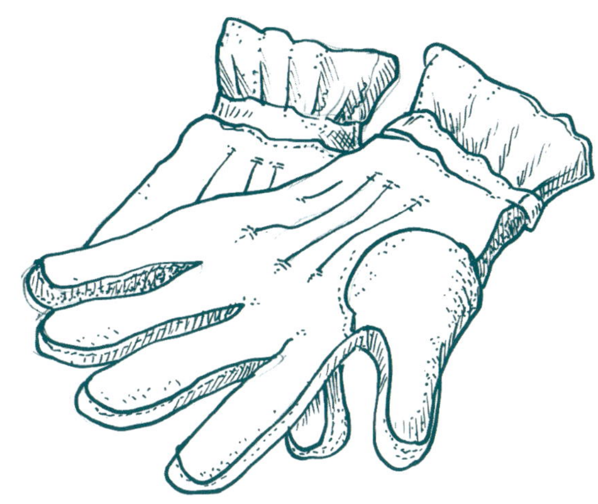

November + December

By November, it's pretty quiet in the garden. If you haven't started cleaning up, you still have some time before the real cold sets in. We'll give you a few last tips on how to put your garden "to bed" for the season.

That is, unless you want to keep on going! November is actually the ideal time to plant garlic for harvest next summer, and to grow mushrooms indoors — we'll explain how. And believe it or not, there is such a thing as "winter gardening" outdoors. We'll give you the highlights and let you entertain the idea.

Final To-Dos

If your raised beds aren't empty by now, they're probably getting pretty sparse. Keep watch on any cool crops that are surviving the frost (a garden-fresh arugula salad this time of year is a real treat!). Once you've cleared out your beds, you can blanket the soil with mulch, straw, leaves, or composted garden scraps for added insulation over the next few months.

After your final harvest, be sure to "winterize" your garden tools so they're in good condition for storage. Remove caked-on dirt and debris with a sponge or brush. For stubborn metal components, try using steel wool or a wire brush. Tighten any loose screws or nuts, and replace them if necessary.

Metal tools with moving parts, such as pruning shears, should be lubricated before storing. Avoid using synthetic or petroleum-based oils, which can transfer onto your plants and into your soil. Instead, check your local nursery for a biodegradable lubricant spray. You can also make homemade spray with linseed, olive, or another vegetable oil. Just pour the oil into a spray bottle and spray a light coating onto your tools, or pour the oil directly onto a rag and then wipe down the tools.

Once your tools are cleaned and lubricated, store them in a spot where they'll stay dry. Small hand tools can be stored blade-side down in a large bucket of sand ("play" sand works fine — it's widely available and inexpensive). The sand will wick away moisture and help keep the tools from rusting.

Take special care to disinfect any tools, as well as containers, stakes, and trellises, that came into contact with diseased plants. Bacteria, fungi, and bug larvae can sometimes overwinter, so taking this extra step (either now or in early spring) will help prevent re-infection next season. Scrub the tool or container with a solution of 1 part household bleach to 9 parts water. Leave the solution on for at least a minute to kill the organisms, then rinse and allow to air dry completely.

One final task that's easy to overlook — but very important — is to put away your garden hose. A hose left outdoors over the winter, with even the slightest amount of water inside, can freeze and expand. This results in either a weakened hose lining or a split hose. Also, leaving a hose connected to a spigot can increase pressure in the water pipes leading into your home, and may eventually cause your water line to leak or even break. So make sure to disconnect your hose from the spigot and drain as much water from it as you can. Store it

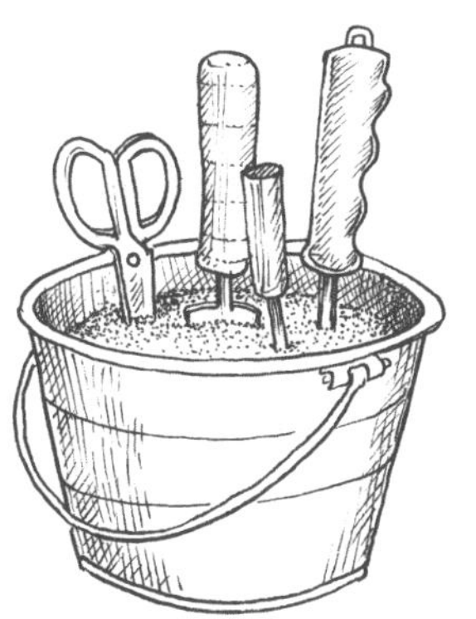

indoors, loosely coiled or hung from a hose reel to prevent kinks. Some homes are equipped with an indoor shut-off valve that drains water from the pipe leading to the outdoor faucet. If you have one of these, utilize it as an extra precaution (you can typically find the valve under a sink, in your basement, or near your water heater or meter).

Planting Garlic

Garlic, as well as shallots, are planted in the fall — just like flower bulbs. They need to settle into cool soil and root before winter arrives. The best time to plant them is early November, about 4 – 6 weeks before the ground freezes.

You'll start with "heads" of garlic that you buy from a garden center, online seed catalog, or farmers market. The heads look like what you buy at the supermarket. So why not just plant the supermarket kind? Because these are often treated with growth inhibitors to prevent sprouting, which defeats the purpose.

When you're ready to plant, break apart the heads and separate the cloves. Set aside the fattest cloves for planting (these will produce the biggest bulbs of garlic come harvest time) and save the smaller cloves for cooking. Loosen your soil and insert the cloves pointed side up, about 3 – 4 inches deep and 4 per square foot. Then cover the cloves with soil. You can add a layer of mulch on top for added protection through the winter. We recommend straw, which can easily be removed in the spring (avoid using hay, which has a tendency to drop seeds that might sprout once temperatures rise).

Your plants will start to emerge in early spring. Each plant will have a stem with leaves, and if it's a hardneck variety, it will form a shoot or "scape" with a small flower bulb. Once the scapes grow above the leaves and start to curl, cut them off 3 – 5 inches below the curl, or as far down as you can without cutting off any leaves. With the scapes removed, the plant will direct its energy toward developing the garlic bulb underground, rather than producing a flower. As an added bonus, you can eat the scapes. They're delicious tossed in salads or blended into pesto sauce.

Sometime in early summer (usually mid-June) your garlic will be ready for harvest. Wait until the bottom leaves of the plants start to turn yellow. To harvest, grasp the stems at the soil level and gently pull, and the bulbs should give way. Or you can use a hand trowel to dig them out, starting from the outside to avoid slicing the bulbs. You'll know you've dug too soon if the cloves are small and haven't yet formed papery skins. You can still eat this "green" garlic in its immature state. Prepare it as you would normal garlic — its flavor will be a bit brighter.

If you end up a mother lode of garlic, you can store it for later use. After harvesting, let the bulbs dry out and cure for a few weeks. Then store them as you would other bulbs and root veggies in a cool, dry, and dark place. You might even hang them from rafters in your garage (especially if you want to keep vampires away).

Winter Gardening

"*Winter* gardening — are you kidding?" No, we're not. Gardening outdoors through the winter isn't for everyone. But if you have the energy and don't mind the cold, then give it a shot!

In Chicago, winter gardening is perhaps better described as winter *survival*. Don't expect your plants to be very prolific through these dark, chilly months. But do aim to keep them alive. You'll need to take extra measures to help insulate them against the cold. You can protect individual plants with cloches, or build larger enclosures such as cold frames or hoop houses to help seal in warmth (see the Beyond the Basics chapter for details). Depending on the weather, and with

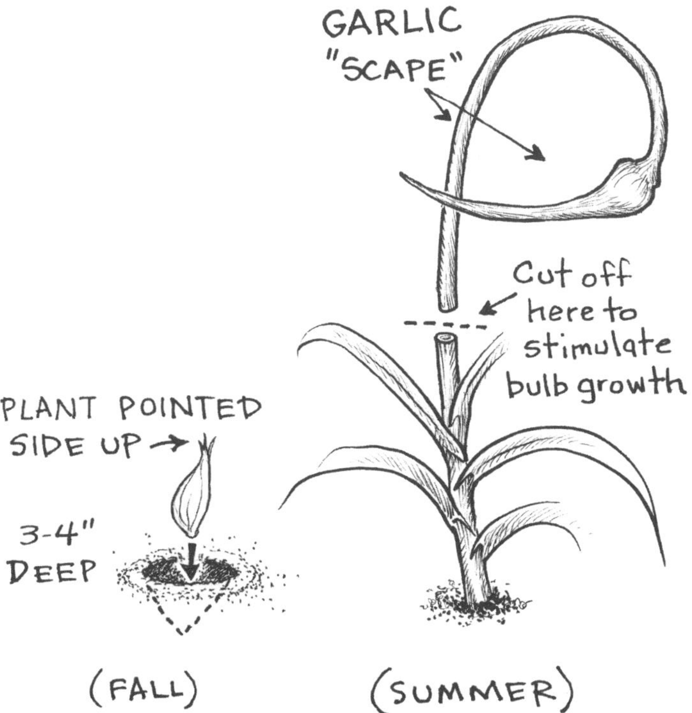

protective devices in place, you can harvest your cold-hardy crops for weeks or perhaps even months to come (see October to review a list of cold-hardy crops).

Winding Down

What to do now that the season's over? Take a well-deserved break. Turn inward. Get cozy with some gardening books or magazines. You might write a postmortem entry in your garden journal. Chronicle what you liked and didn't like, which things grew well, what you might want to try again or do differently next year. Record all this while it's still fresh in your memory. With the holiday season approaching, your mind may soon be elsewhere.

It's normal to feel a sense of loss as your garden bounty starts to dwindle. To help fill this void, you can shop at stores that stock locally grown produce (online stores will deliver to your home—a welcome convenience during a snowstorm). You can also join a "CSA," or Community Supported Agriculture group, where you purchase a share of a regional farm's harvest for the season. It won't be from your backyard, but it will be as close to homegrown food as you can get during this time of year (see the Resources section for more information).

Winter is also an opportune time to connect with other gardeners. Check local gardening organizations to see what classes and events are being offered. Take part in recipes exchanges, "soup swaps," and the like. Relax and enjoy the company of people who share your newfound joy.

And congratulate yourself: you made it through your first gardening season! We hope it was successful and that you learned a lot in the process. And we hope you'll want to do it again next year.

MUSHROOMS

Mushrooms are fun and easy to grow indoors during the winter months. They're different from other vegetables—they're actually a fungus and grow from spores, not seeds. And they don't even need sunlight to grow!

When you're ready to start, look online or at a gardening center for a mushroom "kit." This will include starts or a "spawn" of mushrooms, along with a growing medium (usually compost or straw, depending on what variety of mushroom you choose). You'll spread the mushroom spawn over the growing medium and place it in a warm environment (around 70°) until the mushrooms start to grow. Then you'll move the kit to a dark, cool place (50-60° is ideal) like an unheated basement or mud room, or even a cabinet or closet in an unheated room.

Mushrooms grow in spurts or "flushes." Your first flush will arrive about three weeks after you start your kit. Flushes vary in size. One flush can easily yield dozens of mushrooms. Given the proper growing conditions, your kit should remain productive for many weeks and yield at least one or two more flushes. When the kit is done, you can add the spent compost to your indoor plants or save it for use in your raised beds next spring.

RECIPE BOX

Butternut Squash Soup

Butternut squash is divine just about any way it's prepared. Roasted with onion and garlic, then blended into a smooth, caramely soup — you can't get much better than this. Our recipe uses coconut milk in place of the traditional heavy cream. Serve with warm crusty bread or a grilled cheese sandwich for an extra dose of comfort.

Ingredients

1 medium butternut squash

1 small yellow onion

5 large garlic cloves

2 cups vegetable broth

1 cup unsweetened coconut milk

Olive oil

Salt and freshly ground black pepper

Instructions

Preheat oven to 425°. While oven is preheating, prepare vegetables. Peel squash, remove seeds, and cut into 1-inch cubes.* In a large bowl, combine squash, 2 tablespoons of oil, and a dash of salt and pepper; toss to coat. Spread in a single layer onto a large baking sheet, reserving a corner for onions and garlic.

Peel garlic cloves and leave whole. Peel onion and cut into quarters. Arrange garlic and onions into remaining corner of baking sheet. Drizzle with olive oil, and add a dash of salt and pepper.

Bake vegetables for 20 minutes. Remove garlic and onions and set aside. Stir squash, and return to oven to bake another 20 – 25 minutes; turn with a spatula once or twice during baking to ensure even browning.

In a large saucepan, combine vegetables and ¼ cup of broth; blend with a hand blender until smooth. Alternatively, process vegetables in a blender or food processor in small batches, with a tablespoon or two of broth per batch, until smooth; transfer purée into saucepan. Add remaining broth and coconut milk. Cover and simmer for 20 minutes. For thinner soup, add a few more tablespoons of broth or water.

Serves 6.

* The hard skin of butternut squash can be a bit intimidating. Here's the easiest and safest way to prepare your squash:

1. Wash the squash and pat it dry. Place it sideways on a cutting board. With a large, sharp knife, cut off both ends. Cut the squash in half to separate the thinner "neck" end from the larger bottom end.

2. Stand the neck portion on end. With a sawing motion, slice off the skin from top to bottom. Cut into 1-inch cubes.

3. Stand the bottom half on end. With your knife at an angle, carefully slice off the skin from top to bottom. Depending on how curved the squash is, you may have to slice the top half, then turn the squash over and slice the bottom. Once peeled, cut into half lengthwise and scrape out the seeds and stringy layer of pulp with a spoon. Cut into 1-inch cubes.

RECIPE BOX

Sage Biscuits

We love these no-fuss "drop" biscuits that don't require you to roll out or cut the dough. You just drop mounds of dough onto a baking sheet and watch them rise into free-form shapes as they bake. Crispy on the outside and tender on the inside, with bits of sage in every mouthful...it's hard to stop at just one!

Ingredients

3 cups unbleached all-purpose flour

2 tablespoons sugar

1 tablespoon baking powder

½ teaspoon baking soda

1 teaspoon salt

1½ sticks unsalted butter, chilled and cut into ¼-inch chunks

1 cup buttermilk

12 - 15 fresh sage leaves, cut in chiffonade* (can substitute ¼ cup chopped chives)

Instructions

Preheat oven to 425.° In a large bowl, combine flour, sugar, baking powder, baking soda, and salt. Add butter to dry ingredients. Rub mixture with fingertips until it resembles flakes of coarse meal. Add buttermilk and sage. Stir until dough forms, working with hands if necessary.

Scoop out dough with a measuring cup or by hand, using ¼ cup of dough per biscuit. Drop biscuits onto a large baking sheet, about 2 inches apart. Bake for 15 - 18 minutes, until golden brown. Allow to cool for a few minutes before serving.

Makes 12 biscuits.

* See "Tomato Bruschetta" recipe in July/August for instructions.

Beyond the Basics

We hope you feel inspired after your first year of food gardening. Our guess is that you'll want to learn more from one year to the next. So we'll give you a head start. In this final chapter, we'll share tips on how to support your soil and plant health over the long-term. We'll also give you primers on home composting and starting seeds indoors, and introduce some ways to extend your growing season. Just think of it all as extra credit.

Healthy Soil, Healthy Plants

Your most important job as an organic gardener is caring for your soil. Healthy soil means healthy plants. After your first growing season, your soil typically is still fresh and rich in nutrients. So you don't need to worry about adding fertilizer or other soil "amendments" at this point.

Over time your soil conditions may change, depending on the growing conditions of each particular season. It's best to think of soil maintenance as a long-term practice. Here we'll outline some fundamental techniques you can adopt early on to help support the ongoing health of your garden.

Compost is the best all-purpose soil amendment. It improves your soil's texture and ability to hold water, and provides a full spectrum of nutrients that aren't found in commercial fertilizers. Plants absorb nutrients from compost gradually over time. They take what they need, when they need it. While you can't really "over-use" compost, you should be selective about how and when you apply it. The most important time to add compost to your soil is at the start of the growing season. A little goes a long way — a 1-inch layer on top of the soil is sufficient to boost the health of new plantings. You can also add a thin layer of compost around the base of your plants every few weeks throughout the growing season.

Alternatively, you can make compost "tea" to use for periodic supplements. The tea-brewing process extracts and can even multiply nutrients and beneficial bacteria from compost. In a liquid form, these nutrients are quickly absorbed by plants. Compost tea is particularly useful for containers with limited capacity.

To brew the tea, combine 1 pound of compost per 1 gallon of water in a large bucket. Make sure to use mature compost that smells sweet and earthy (a foul odor means the compost has decomposed without enough oxygen and won't have many beneficial microbes). Store the bucket away from extreme temperatures, and stir the mixture daily for at least five days. Then use cheesecloth or burlap to strain the liquid into another bucket or watering can. Pour the tea around the base of your plants as you would regular water.

Over time, and depending on what crops you grow, your soil may become depleted of certain nutrients. Adding fertilizer to your soil can help replenish nutrients that plants have consumed. All plants require nitrogen, phosphorus, and potassium in order to thrive (plants feed on other nutrients as well, but these are the most heavily consumed). Different plants use these essential nutrients, commonly referred to as "N-P-K," to varying degrees. Leafy plants consume high amounts of nitrogen, fruiting and flowering plants use lots of phosphorus, and root crops like a lot of potassium. Legumes actually add nitrogen back into the soil.

How do you know if fertilizer is necessary? First, observe your plants for signs of a nutrient deficiency (see the "Essential Plant Nutrients" table for details). If they appear healthy, there's no need to intervene. And if they show symptoms, add fertilizer accordingly. One application during the growing season is usually sufficient to support the health of existing plants.

Determining what nutrients your soil needs may involve some guesswork. If you're uncertain, you probably won't go wrong using a multi-purpose vegetable fertilizer with a balance of nutrients. You can also keep a log of what you've planted and where to help gauge your soil's nutrient content. For example, if you've grown salad greens in the same spot for the last few years, that area of soil might benefit from a nitrogen boost. In this case, you could add a nitrogen-rich fertilizer at the start of the next growing season as a preventive measure.

When shopping for fertilizer, you'll find products made from a variety of plant, animal, and mineral based materials. Look for an organic product containing the OMRI® label (this means it's been quality-assured by the Organic Materials Review Institute). Also refer to the "guaranteed analysis" section of the package to identify the percentage of N-P-K nutrients. So for example, a label that reads "5-10-10" means the fertilizer contains 5% nitrogen, 10% phosphorus, and 10% potassium.

You'll also have the choice between granular and liquid forms. Granular fertilizer releases slowly into the soil and requires the help of microbes to break it down and make its nutrients available to plants. Wait until at least late spring to apply granular fertilizer, once the soil has had time to warm up and microbes are active. Liquid fertilizer is readily absorbed by plants, so it can be applied in early spring even before the soil has warmed. For any product, always take care to follow the application instructions listed on the package.

With a bit of planning, you may be able to reduce or altogether avoid the need for fertilizer. As you choose what to grow from one season to the next, try to include a variety of plants. Of course you'll have your favorites (we all do!). But add some new things to the mix, too. Crop diversity helps strengthen your garden ecosystem. It's an organic practice that's simple and effective.

ESSENTIAL PLANT NUTRIENTS (N-P-K)

	Nitrogen (N)	Phosphorus (P)	Potassium (K)
Function	Promotes green leafy growth.	Promotes flowering, fruiting, and strong root growth.	Promotes strong roots and stems. Increases resistance to disease, heat, and cold. Supports overall plant health.
Common deficiency signs	Yellow-green foliage, often occurring first in older leaves. New leaves are reduced in size, or have yellow or brown edges.	Stems and leaf veins are purple. Plants mature slowly and yields are low.	Low yields and poor resistance to disease. Mottled, speckled, or curled leaves, and weak stems.
Common organic sources of fertilizer	• Animal manure • Blood meal • Bone meal • Compost • Cottonseed meal • Feather meal • Fish meal • Legumes • Worm castings	• Animal manure • Bat guano (manure) • Bone meal • Colloidal phosphate • Compost • Cottonseed meal • Fish meal • Rock phosphate	• Alfalfa green manure • Compost • Granite meal • Greensand • Kelp meal • Seaweed • Wood ashes

Another age-old organic technique is crop rotation. This means not growing the same kind of plant in the same spot year after year. Moving your crops around helps replenish soil nutrients and confuses insects who like to feed on a particular vegetable or plant family. You can rotate your crops in a variety of ways.

Rotating according to plant family helps deter pests that favor a specific vegetable or plant family. Insects often leave eggs or larvae in the soil near their host plant, which can overwinter and emerge in the spring, looking to feed on that same veggie. So if you had an infestation of cabbage worms this year, plant your cabbage in a different spot next season. Then any larvae that survive the winter and appear in the spring will have a hard time finding their favorite food.

You can also rotate according to which part of the plant you harvest. This helps build soil fertility and resistance to disease. A simple method is to follow the sequence "leaf, root, flower, fruit." If you have multiple beds, you can plant one with leaf crops, one with root crops, and so on — and then switch them around from year to year. Or if you have a single raised bed, you can group like-crops together in different sections of the bed, and then rotate the sections.

Alternatively, you can plant in succession. In other words, promptly remove plants that are finished or past their peak, and replace them with new seeds or transplants from a different plant family or group. By planting in immediate succession, you can accomplish at least one rotation within a single growing season and maximize the productivity of your garden. Succession planting is a particularly useful technique if you have just one raised bed.

And it never hurts to add peas and beans into the mix, especially in spots where you've grown leafy greens. Remember, legumes add nitrogen back into the soil.

We admit, crop rotation may be easier said than done. It can be challenging if you have limited space or like to grow the same things from one year to the next. For repeat crops, you can try rotating between your raised beds and containers. Do what's practical and what makes the most sense in your garden.

EDIBLE PLANT FAMILIES

Common names + (botanical names)

Aster/Sunflower (Asteraceae)
- Endive
- Globe artichokes
- Jerusalem artichokes
- Lettuce
- Sunflowers

Beet/Goosefoot (Chenopodiaceae)
- Beets
- Spinach
- Swiss chard

Cabbage/Mustard (Brassicaceae)
- Arugula
- Bok choi
- Broccoli
- Brussels sprouts
- Cabbage
- Cauliflower
- Collards
- Cress
- Horseradish
- Kale
- Kohlrabi
- Mustard greens
- Radishes
- Rutabagas
- Turnips

Carrot (Umbelliferae)
- Anise
- Carrots
- Celery
- Chervil
- Cilantro
- Dill
- Fennel
- Lovage
- Parsley
- Parsnips

Corn/Grass (Gramineae)
- Corn
- Rye
- Wheat

Legume/Pulse (Fabaceae)
- Beans
- Peas

Lily (Liliaceae)
- Asparagus
- Okra

Mint (Lamiaceae)
- Basil
- Lavender
- Mint
- Oregano
- Rosemary
- Sage

Nasturtium (Tropaeolum)
- Nasturtiums

Nightshade (Solanaceae)
- Eggplant
- Peppers
- Potatoes
- Tomatillos
- Tomatoes

Onion/Allium (Alliaceae)
- Chives
- Garlic
- Leeks
- Onions
- Shallots

Rose (Rosaceae)
- Strawberries

Squash/Gourd (Cucurbitaceae)
- Cucumbers
- Gourds
- Melons
- Pumpkins
- Summer squash
- Winter squash

PLANT GROUPS FOR FERTILITY ROTATION

Leaf
- Basil
- Fennel
- Cabbage
- Celery
- Cilantro
- Collards
- Dill
- Garlic
- Leeks
- Lettuce
- Mustard greens
- Onions
- Parsley
- Swiss chard

Root
- Beets
- Carrots
- Jerusalem artichokes
- Parsnips
- Potatoes
- Radishes
- Rutabagas
- Turnips

Flower
- Annual flowers
- Artichokes
- Broccoli
- Buckwheat
- Cauliflower

Fruit
- Beans
- Corn
- Cucumbers
- Eggplant
- Gourds
- Melons
- Peas
- Peppers
- Pumpkins
- Squash
- Tomatillos
- Tomatoes

Home Composting

You'll always need compost for your garden. So why not make your own? Homemade compost is often richer in nutrients than store-bought varieties. And composting is the most sustainable way to dispose of your garden and kitchen waste. To grow your plants, harvest them, and then return the by-products to the soil is a process that brings your garden full circle.

There are many ways to compost — with varying degrees of efficiency — but the end result is the same. All plant matter breaks down eventually. When you compost at home, you're simply encouraging this natural process to happen more quickly, and in a concentrated form.

Composting can be as little or as much work as you're willing to put into it. "Passive" approaches to composting require minimal effort on your part. You simply collect the waste in a concentrated area and let nature take its course. After that, you don't intervene. Time, moisture, oxygen, and microorganisms do all the work. "Active" composting methods involve physical intervention to help accelerate decomposition. Practically, this means turning the compost and maintaining moisture levels.

In general, the more active your approach, the sooner you'll get "finished" compost that's fully broken down and ready for use in your garden. The most active methods take at least a couple months to produce finished compost. If you don't mind waiting awhile longer (or if you're feeling lazy), you can opt for a more passive style. Even if it takes a year, you'll still end up with usable compost.

To house your compost, you'll need an outdoor space large enough for a dedicated pile or enclosure. Set aside a 4 x 4-foot area if possible. Compost piles actually generate heat during the decomposition process, but only if they have sufficient mass and volume. A 4 x 4-foot pile (up to 4 feet tall) will hold enough volume to maintain the heat needed for rapid decomposition. A pile smaller than 3 x 3 feet won't retain heat as well and may dry out quickly. If you build your pile larger than 5 x 5 feet, oxygen will have a hard time reaching the center (where all the heat and action takes place), and you might end up with anaerobic — and very smelly — compost.

Your compost pile can be just what its name suggests: an uncontained pile or heap. This is the most "open" form of compost collection, requiring little set-up time and zero expense. The downside to an open heap is that it tends to spread out and doesn't stay very hot, so decomposition is slower. Your neighbors might also find your sprawling pile a bit unsightly.

Containing your compost in an enclosure helps build volume and maintain heat. Homemade enclosures are inexpensive and easy to construct. Our favorite method is to stretch hardware cloth or chicken wire into a circle or around four corner fence posts, and secure with wire or twist ties. You also can use stacked cinderblocks or untreated wood palettes to form a bin. These kinds of enclosures are still open, allowing oxygen and water to reach the pile, and giving you physical access to the pile.

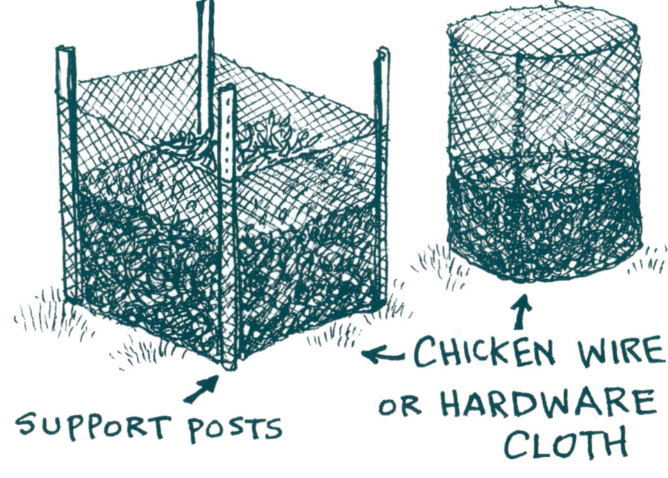

Alternatively, you can opt for a more "closed" composting vessel. The most economical form is a large trash can with holes drilled in it for ventilation. You can also purchase plastic compost bins with lids, as well as "tumblers" with built-in mechanisms designed to ease the turning process. Closed vessels help discourage furry foragers, but they often have small capacities, and pre-fabricated bins can be expensive.

Before you start composting, check your local ordinances to confirm what's permitted in your area. The city of Chicago allows for residential composting as long as the pile doesn't create odor or dust and doesn't attract rodents or pests. A well managed compost pile will do neither. If you're composting only landscape and garden waste, you can use an open system. If you're adding food and kitchen waste to your pile, local ordinances may require you to put a cover on your composting vessel to deter rodents.

So what exactly can you compost? Any plant matter that's not diseased: vegetable scraps, grass, newspaper, wood chips, and coffee grounds (some coffee shops give these away for free!), to name a few. You'll be surprised by how many things you normally throw away can actually be composted. "Brown" materials that are dried or dead (newspaper, sawdust, old leaves, etc.) supply carbon to your pile, while "green" materials that are moist and recently alive (fruit and vegetable pieces, grass clippings, fresh leaves, etc.) supply nitrogen. Theories abound on the optimal proportions of compost ingredients. Don't worry about getting the mixture "right." As long as you add a variety of ingredients, both brown and green, your compost should turn out just fine.

As for what *not* to put in your compost — avoid any synthetic materials, which don't break down easily and can leach unwanted chemical by-products. And refrain from adding animal products (eggshells are okay) and manure from meat-eating animals, which can harbor harmful bacteria and create foul odors. Also avoid adding diseased and pest-laden plants to your pile, as well as weeds that have gone to seed. You don't want any of these pesky things reappearing in your garden.

Before adding materials to your compost pile, cut them into small pieces so they break down faster. Use either a spade fork or shovel to turn (or chop, or stir) an open pile. As you turn, make sure to bring materials from the edges toward the center, and keep any fresh food scraps covered. In general, the more often you turn your compost, the more quickly it will mature. Even if you fill your bin all the way to the top, the pile will compress and get smaller as it decomposes.

Check the moisture level of your pile every so often. It should be the consistency of a wrung-out sponge. If it's too dry, add water or more green materials. And if it's too moist, add more brown materials or turn the pile to aerate and help it dry out. The pile should also smell sweet and earthy. If it has an unpleasant or ammonia-like odor, then it's probably decomposing anaerobically and needs to be turned more.

What you can compost

- Cardboard (shredded)
- Coffee grounds & filters
- Eggshells (crushed)
- Fruit & vegetable scraps
- Grass clippings
- Hedge trimmings
- Leaves
- Newspaper (shredded)
- Nutshells
- Pine cones (chopped)
- Potting soil
- Poultry manure
- Sawdust (from untreated wood)
- Spent flowers & plants
- Straw
- Tea bags
- Twigs (shredded)
- Wood chips (from untreated wood)

What NOT to compost

- Bakery products
- Branches
- Cat litter
- Cat or dog manure
- Cheese
- Cooking oil or grease
- Dairy products
- Diseased or pest-laden plants
- Eggs
- Glossy paper
- Meat or fish scraps
- Plate scraps
- Weeds with seeds

In Chicago, you can compost outdoors for most of the year. Once your pile freezes (usually in late fall or early winter, depending on temperatures), you won't be able to turn it. Take a break at this point. The pile won't be decomposing much during the winter, anyway. As soon as it thaws in the spring, you can start up again.

Finished compost will always be at the bottom of your pile. You need to dig deep to find the good stuff. If you like, you can cut a small door at the bottom of your bin for easy access. Ideally your mature compost will have the texture and color of crumbled chocolate cake. It's okay if you find an occasional chunk like a twig, pit, or pine cone. You can sift these things out and remove them. But if the compost is still very chunky, it needs more time.

You can use your "black gold" in a variety of ways. Add it as a top layer in your raised beds in the spring or periodically throughout the growing season. A little compost goes a long way. Usually an inch or so, spread evenly over the area, is enough. If you have a surplus, store it in plastic bags or trash cans for later in the season or for new soil mixtures, or sprinkle it around landscape plantings (annuals, perennials, shrubs, etc.). You can also make compost "tea" for use as a liquid supplement for plants in containers or beds with limited capacity (look back to "Healthy Soil, Healthy Plants" to learn how).

Extending Your Season

So far we've advised you to follow Mother Nature's cues when deciding how soon to plant in the spring and when to call it quits in the fall. But you can actually "cheat" and extend your growing season on both ends. With the help of protective covers, you can plant earlier in the spring and grow later in the fall (and possibly on into the winter). As an added bonus, covering your plants helps keep pests at bay.

Cloches and floating row covers are handy tools that may suit your needs just fine (look back to April's "Protective Devices" section to review). Cloches can be used to cover individual plants, while floating row covers can be stretched over multiple plants or entire garden beds. Both devices help warm air and soil temperatures and can prevent frost from coming into contact with your plants. If you're using a cloche without an opening, make sure to remove it periodically for ventilation.

For a sturdier enclosure, try using a cold frame or hoop house. Either requires a bit of time and effort to construct, but they both offer heavy-duty protection and can last many seasons with proper care.

A cold frame works like a cloche, but is heavier and has a larger capacity. It consists of a box with solid sides, a glass or Plexiglass lid that opens and closes, and an open bottom that rests on the soil. A cold frame can be placed directly over a portion of your raised bed and cover several plants at a time. The lid should be propped open during the day as the weather permits to provide air circulation to plants. Cold frames usually aren't over 12 – 18 inches tall, so they're most useful when plants are small. They're especially well suited for protecting newly transplanted seedlings in the spring.

A hoop house is an enclosure made to fit your raised bed, transforming it into a kind of miniature greenhouse. Materials for a hoop house are inexpensive, and the device itself is easy to build. To make the frame, use two pieces of ½-inch PVC pipe, 5 – 10 feet each in length, or at least two feet longer than the area you're covering (longer pipes will give you a taller frame). Bend each pipe into an upside-down "U" and anchor it diagonally into opposite corners of your bed. Then secure the pipes together where they intersect with plastic wire ties.

For a different shape, you can bend each pipe into an arch at the short ends of your bed, and connect them with a third pipe cut to the length of the bed. Drill holes in the top of your arched pipes and at both ends of your third pipe. Then thread a wire tie through the holes to fasten the pipes together, or secure them with a bolt or screw.

After assembling your frame, cover it with protective material. Floating row cover material guards well against light frost and transitional temperatures, while clear plastic offers stronger protection. Make sure to anchor your cover to the ground, and allow for an opening so you can ventilate and tend your crops as needed.

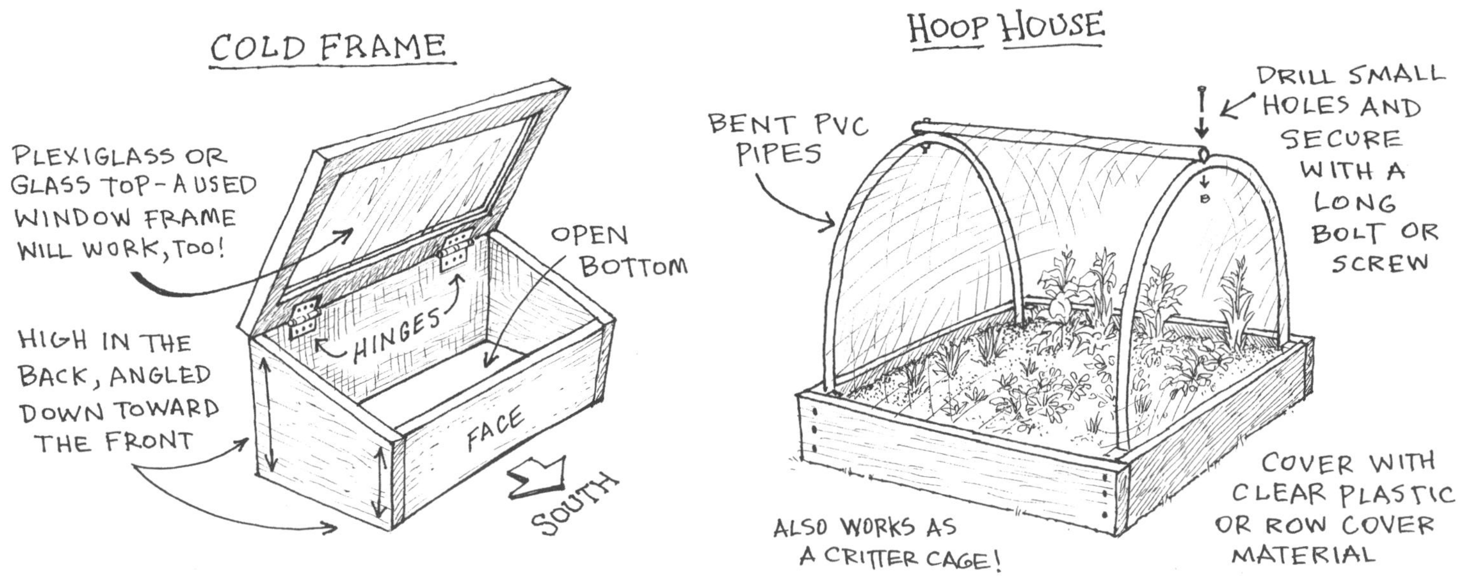

Starting Seeds Indoors

Experienced gardeners often like to start seeds indoors in late winter or early spring. Plants are grown indoors until soil and air temperatures are warm enough to transplant them outside — April or May, depending on the crop. "Seed starting," as the process is called, can be done to get a jump on the growing season before outdoor conditions would allow, or to save money that you'd otherwise spend on seedlings. It also gives you a means to grow rare varieties of fruits and veggies that are sold in seed catalogs, but not at your local nursery.

Many crops can be started indoors. If you're eager to get growing as soon as possible in the spring, lettuce and other greens are a good choice. These crops can handle cool weather and can be transplanted in the ground right as the soil thaws. Since you'll be starting from seedlings rather than seeds, your harvest will come a few weeks earlier.

On the other hand, hot crop favorites like tomatoes, eggplants, and peppers can't be put into the ground safely until late May. Since these plants take a long time to mature (17-19 weeks), they're commonly purchased as seedlings rather than sown in the garden directly from seed. Growing your own seedlings can be a fun alternative to buying them at a garden center. By the time you transplant your homegrown seedlings outside, they'll be at about the same stage in their growth cycle as store-bought plants. You won't be getting a head start like you would with cool season greens, but you'll save money and have the chance to grow varieties that you might not find at conventional nurseries, including varieties sold from online sources.

A few crops don't take well to transplanting — in particular, beans, melons, squash, and cucumbers. For these, we suggest direct seeding outdoors. Seeds for root vegetables should be sown directly outdoors as well.

Use the recommendation from your seed packet or seed catalog to determine how early to start your seeds indoors. If the seed packet doesn't provide this information, we advise starting in late February or March, 8 – 12 weeks in advance of when it's safe to plant outside.

When scouting a site for your indoor seed starting operation, choose a place that's relatively warm like a basement or heated garage. A spare closet, cabinet, or extra shelves can also work well if you have limited space. Once your seeds germinate and start to grow, you'll need to locate them near a south-facing window or near supplemental light (we'll explain what this means in a bit). Also consider that you'll be dealing with soil and water, and the potential for mess. So pick an area that's easy to clean, or make sure to protect carpets or other surfaces that could be easily damaged.

There's lots of fancy "gear" available for seed starting. Don't worry about this for now. We recommend starting small and simple with just a few supplies: containers, soil, and some inexpensive fluorescent lights.

You don't need to look far to find suitable containers. Recycled food containers like yogurt cups or small milk cartons cut to size will work fine. Make sure to wash them first and poke a few holes in the bottom for drainage. You can also re-use old nursery pots, as long as you scrub them with a mild bleach and water solution to kill any bacteria. Ideally your pots should be at least 4 inches wide and 3 inches deep for strong root development. And in addition, you'll need a tray with tall sides to place underneath your pots. The tray will catch extra water and ease moving the pots from one place to another.

For your planting medium, you won't use the same soil as you would outside in your raised beds. You'll need to purchase an organic "soilless" seed starting mix instead. Seed starting mix is sterile (so it's free of disease organisms) and is formulated with very fine materials to absorb water and give seedlings maximum support. Look for organic seed starting mix at your local nursery or grocery store, or order it online.

Once you have all your materials, find a workspace where you can spread everything out and get messy. Pour your seed starting mix into a large bucket or pan. Add some water and work the mix with your hands until it has a mud-like consistency (it should hold together in your hand if you make a fist). Then fill your pots to the brim. Plant your seeds to the depth listed on the seed packet and cover them gently with soil. Label the pots so you don't lose track of what you've planted and when. Arrange the pots onto your tray when you're finished.

Light is not required during the germination period. But the soil does need to stay moist (just moist, not wet) and relatively warm in order for seeds to sprout. Use a spray bottle to lightly mist the soil. In addition, you can place a lid over the pots or cover them with plastic wrap to help retain moisture. Most vegetable seeds require temperatures between 55 – 75° to germinate (65 – 75° for hot crops and 55 – 65° for cool crops). Some germinate very quickly, while others can take 10 or more days. Check your seed packet to confirm the days to germination for each particular crop, so you'll know what to anticipate.

After your seedlings emerge, remove any covers and place the pots near a source of bright light. The plants will need 12-16 hours of light per day in order to grow strong and healthy. Yes, this is a lot of light. Adequate light is *really* important. Your plants will become spindly and prone to disease without enough light exposure. A south-facing window will give them a good start, but unfortunately at our northern latitude, natural light alone is rarely sufficient.

This is where the supplemental light comes in. Believe it or not, your seedlings will grow best with the help of broad-spectrum fluorescent lights. You can rig up a system using clamp lights or suspend tube lighting from the ceiling with chains (supplies are relatively inexpensive either way). Since fluorescent lights are cool, you can place them very close to your plants without burning the leaves. Position the lights 1-2 inches above the tops of the plants, and raise the lights with the plants as they get taller. It may seem unnatural to blast your little sprouts like this, but it really is crucial to your success.

You'll need to keep your soil moist, but not soaking wet, as the seedlings grow. It's best to allow the surface of the soil to dry out a little between waterings. Use your finger to test the soil for moisture. If you press half an inch down and the soil is dry, then it's time to water. Remember to water the soil and not the leaves. An alternative to watering from the top is to fill your tray with an inch or so of water and let the plants absorb moisture from the bottom. This technique is useful in a tight space or if you can't easily get under your lighting system to access the plants. Watering from the bottom also helps prevent excess moisture on the plants themselves, which can lead to disease.

Too much moisture on your seedlings, as well as stagnant air and high humidity, can harbor a fungal disease called "damping off." The fungi attack seedlings at the soil level, cutting off water and nutrient supplies and killing the plants. You'll know your plants are affected if they form a dark ring around the stem at the soil level and suddenly keel over (unfortunately, affected plants rarely recover). You can help prevent damping off by providing good air circulation and not soaking the soil.

Since seed starting mixes don't contain nutrients, you'll need to give the soil a nutrient boost every so often to keep your plants growing strong and healthy. Wait until the seedlings are about 2 inches tall, and then apply fertilizer every 10-14 days. Use liquid fertilizer rather than granular, since nutrients are more readily absorbed from liquid. Fish emulsion is our favorite (package instructions will indicate how much water to add).

In a matter of weeks, your seedlings will be ready to move outside. Once the average outdoor temperature is warm enough for your particular crop, you can start the "hardening off" process. This consists of gradually acclimating your plants to outdoor growing conditions — sunlight, wind, temperature fluctuations, and possibly rain — so they don't go into shock when you transplant them. Take the plants outside on a warm day and set them in the shade for a few hours. Then bring them back inside at night. Continue this over the course of a week or two, gradually exposing the plants to longer periods of sunlight each day until they're outside all day. At the end of the hardening off period, your plants should be adjusted to outdoor conditions — and ready to transplant and thrive in your garden!

Resources

CLIMATE INFORMATION

State Climatologist Office for Illinois
www.isws.illinois.edu/atmos/statecli/
Comprehensive resource for up-to-date climate information in Illinois, including frost maps and dates.

COMMUNITY GARDENING

American Community Gardening Association (ACGA)
www.communitygarden.org
Member organization dedicated to building community gardens and sustainable communities in the United States and Canada.

Connecting Chicago Community Gardens (CCCG)
www.facebook.com/ConnectingChicagoCommunityGardens
Online forum for Chicago-based community gardeners to network and share information.

Peterson Garden Project (PGP) | www.petersongarden.org
Community garden program and educational resource located on Chicago's north side.

FOOD PANTRIES & DONATIONS

Greater Chicago Food Depository | www.chicagosfoodbank.org/site/PageServer?pagename=lb_need_agencylocator
"Agency Locator" tool lists food pantries in Cook County, searchable by zip code.

FOOD PRESERVATION

National Center for Home Food Preservation | nchfp.uga.edu
Gives current research-based information on all methods of home food preservation.

INTENSIVE GARDENING

All-New Square Foot Gardening by Mel Bartholomew. Cool Springs Press, 2005.
Seminal book on "square foot" gardening, with in-depth information on raised beds and intensive growing techniques.

"Kitchen Garden Planner" by Gardener's Supply Company.
http://www.gardeners.com/Kitchen-Garden-Planner/kgp_home,default,pg.html
Online tool to help organize garden layout. Determines how many veggies to plant per square foot, plus generates illustrations and growing instructions.

LOCAL FOOD

Local Harvest | www.localharvest.org
Lists farmers markets, family farms, and other sources of sustainably grown food, organized by region.

Slow Food Chicago | www.slowfoodchicago.org
Hosts events promoting sustainable food producers and purveyors in the Chicago area. Also lists farmers markets and CSA (Community Supported Agriculture) farms.

ONLINE GARDENING TOOLS

Folia | www.myfolia.com
Provides free software for tracking the progress of your garden, plus lots of helpful information and opportunities to connect with other food gardeners.

PEST & DISEASE MANAGEMENT

"Common Problems for Vegetable Crops" by University of Illinois Extension. | urbanext.illinois.edu/vegproblems
Lists full array of common insects and diseases. Includes photos and descriptions for easy diagnosis, plus tips for management.

SEED SOURCES

Our favorite seed catalogs:

Baker Creek Heirloom Seeds | www.rareseeds.com

Bounty Beyond Belief | www.bbbseed.com

Botanical Interests | www.botanicalinterests.com

Renee's Garden | www.reneesgarden.com

Seed Savers Exchange | www.seedsavers.org

Territorial Seeds | www.territorialseed.com

Home Garden Seed Association | www.ezfromseed.org
Member organization committed to promoting gardening from seed. Provides seasonal information for home gardeners, as well as seed catalog listings.

VEGETABLE GARDENING

"Watch Your Garden Grow" by University of Illinois Extension.
urbanext.illinois.edu/veggies/
Quick reference guide for growing vegetables in Illinois region.

BOOKS WE RECOMMEND

The Edible Front Yard: The Mow-Less, Grow-More Plan for a Beautiful, Bountiful Garden by Ivette Soler. Timber Press, 2011.

Farmer John's Cookbook: The Real Dirt on Vegetables by John Peterson. Gibbs-Smith, 2009.

Grocery Gardening: Planting, Preparing and Preserving Fresh Food by Jean Ann Van Krevelen. Cool Springs Press, 2010.

Grow Great Grub: Organic Food from Small Spaces by Gayla Trail. Clarkson Potter, 2010.

Pick Fresh Cookbook: Creating Irresistible Dishes from the Best Seasonal Produce by the Editors of Cooking Light Magazine and Mary Beth Burner Shaddix. Oxmoor House, 2013.

Vertical Vegetables and Fruit: Creative Gardening Techniques for Growing Up in Small Spaces by Rhonda Massingham Hart. Storey Publishing, 2011.

Your Farm in the City: An Urban-Dweller's Guide to Growing Food and Raising Animals by Lisa Taylor and the Gardeners of Seattle Tilth. Black Dog & Leventhal, 2011.

OUR FAVORITE MAGAZINES

Edible Chicago

Organic Gardening

Mother Earth News

Urban Farm

BIBLIOGRAPHY

Bartholomew, Mel. *All-New Square Foot Gardening.* Cool Springs Press, 2005.

Coyne, Kelly, and Erik Knutzen. *The Urban Homestead: Your Guide to Self-Sufficient Living in the Heart of the City.* Process Media, 2010.

Elliott, Carl, and Rob Peterson. *The Maritime Northwest Garden Guide.* Seattle Tilth, 2000.

Kujawski, Jennifer and Ron. *Week-by-Week Vegetable Gardener's Handbook.* Storey Publishing, 2010.

Seattle Tilth. *Organic Gardening Field Guide,* Seattle Tilth, 2013.

"Seed Buying 101: A Seed Gardener's Glossary." Home Garden Seed Association. http://ezfromseed.org/files/2012-spring-press.pdf.